Gary Glitter w[...] Oxfordshire. [...] fifteen and went on to tour in various bands and under various names until becoming Gary Glitter in 1972. Since then he has sold over 18 million records around the world. His many hits include 'Leader of the Gang', 'Do You Wanna Touch Me (Oh Yeah)' and 'Rock 'n' Roll, Parts 1 & 2'. After a period out of the limelight, the Gary Glitter Gang Show now tours in the UK every Christmas at venues which include Wembley Arena and Birmingham NEC. During 1990 Gary Glitter also toured as Eric 'Rubberlegs' de Vene in the hit musical *A Slice of Saturday Night*. When he is not on board his yacht, he lives in a village in Somerset.

LEADER

The Autobiography

GARY GLITTER
with
Lloyd Bradley

WARNER BOOKS

A *Warner* Book

First published in Great Britain in 1991
by Ebury Press
First published by Warner Books in 1992

Copyright © Machmain Limited 1991

A CIP catalogue record for this book is available from the British Library.

ISBN 0 7515 0009 7

Typesetting by
Edna A. Moore, 𝍫 Tek-Art, Addiscombe, Croydon, Surrey

Printed in England by Clays Ltd, St Ives plc

Warner Books
A Division of
Little, Brown and Company (UK) Limited
165 Great Dover Street
London SE1 4YA

To the Gang

Contents

Acknowledgements

As the Leader I must bring to the reader's attention that it is doubtful that I would ever have been in the position to tell my story if I had not had the support and encouragement of many Gang members throughout the world (and they *all* know who they are) who shared the incredible 'highs' and indescribable 'lows' that I have experienced in the epic saga of my life so far. Special thanks for my family, friends, Mike Leander, Alan Gee and, of course, Jef Hanlon. I would also like to acknowledge the patience, dedication and sensitivity constantly exhibited by Lloyd Bradley during our time together writing this book.

Thanks for being there everybody.

Prologue

Twenty years ago I was thumbing through a copy of *Melody Maker* and came across a feature that looked back on the music of the late fifties and early sixties: it ran in two parts over consecutive issues. I can't remember now if I even read the feature or not, but the title of it changed my life. It was called 'Rock 'n' Roll, Parts 1 & 2'. When I took that as the theme and the hook for the song I was struggling to write a couple of months later, it was as if the tumblers of a lock I'd been trying to pick for the previous ten years finally fell into place and the safe door swung open.

What lay beyond that door was an adventure of fairytale – and in some cases comic book – proportions. It took me to the top of the charts in three continents; to the best hotels and restaurants in the world, in the company of some of the planet's most beautiful women and biggest stars; and to the role of lord of the manor on an estate in Hampshire. It was a lifestyle as far removed as is possible from what went before – years of barely scratching a living from singing the rock 'n' roll I loved.

Writing this book was probably the first time I've

ever reflected on my life as a whole, and it wasn't until I'd nearly finished it that I realised most of my life has been spent on the outside of the supposed 'in-crowds'. And by the time I'd got to the end I was satisfied I wouldn't have had it any other way. Every time I've been kept out of somebody else's gang I've gone on to form my own, and usually had a lot more fun. With the possible exception of a couple of very low periods, I've enjoyed my life immensely.

I hope it's as good to read as it has been to live.

1
Born Leader

My earliest memory is of what I took to be a hospital, full of fat ladies eating cabbage and hard-boiled eggs. It was actually a workhouse-cum-maternity home in the Oxfordshire countryside, for women who had become pregnant outside of marriage. I was two and a half, and staying there because my younger brother Tony was being born. Although it wasn't as grim as a genuine workhouse, it wasn't the most luxurious place either. The living quarters were spartan – basically furnished dormitories and a few rooms that were more like cells. The washrooms were communal. Everywhere smelled of disinfectant. And meals – which seemed to be nothing other than hard-boiled eggs and cabbage – were taken at long wooden tables in a huge hall.

Even at that age I can remember feeling there was a stigma attached to being there, yet there was obviously a demand. This was 1946, a year after the Second World War ended; there was a great shortage of men in Britain, and girls were having affairs with virtually any male who was capable. There were so many unmarried mothers that this country is now full of forty-five to fifty-year-olds who have never known their fathers! The girls' parents, brought up in the Victorian era, often reacted to what they saw as shame being brought to the family by sending the girl away. Establishments like the home in Oxfordshire were the only places they could go. They'd do light assembly or sewing work in return for their keep, and stay on aftewards for however long it took to fix up somewhere to go.

I'd been born there, too. My mother wasn't married to my father, and my grandmother had thrown her out because the pregnancy came after a family scandal surrounding the birth of my half-brother David. Ten years previously my mother and her sister Ryne were both seeing the same man, the son of a wealthy local landowner, and both became pregnant at the same time. Gran decided that as Auntie Ryne was the eldest, she was the one who should marry him. Ryne moved away after that and wouldn't have anything to do with Mum – she still doesn't talk to me, which I find a bid odd because it was hardly my fault. Mum was only in her early twenties then, and Gran let her and David live at home; but when she got involved with my father, who was married, it was too much for my grandmother. Mum left David behind, had me in the home and spent two and a half years working as a live-in domestic for any family that would take me as part of the package. When Tony was born, though, we were taken back into the family home. It was as if Gran had decided that Mum had paid her penance.

Tony and I have the same father, a man by the name of Albert who was manager of the local aluminium factory. According to neighbourhood gossip, he had about six daughters around the area as well. I never knew him. I've never found out his surname, and I don't know if he's still alive or not; he never showed any particular interest in me or my brother, either. Also, because of Gran's old-fashioned attitude towards anything to do with sex, Tony and I were always told not to tell the truth about our situation. I made up a very romantic tale about my father being a wartime Spitfire pilot who'd been shot down over Germany. As a schoolboy, the fiction was so much more attractive to me that I stuck to it strongly – enough to start believing it. I certainly had little interest in a man who was no more exciting than a factory boss and who had another family to his name.

I was born Paul Gadd on 8 May 1944. The after-effects of the war were very much in evidence during my early childhood. Rationing was still in force – there weren't any sweets in the shops until I was about six; clothing was in short supply; there were still gas masks hanging up in every home and, because of the lack of men, Britain had become a very matriarchal society. This was definitely the case in our family. My grandmother was a tiny woman, prone to plumpness – which is probably where I get it from – and, ever since I can remember, with completely white hair. But she was a tyrant. In a household which consisted of practically all women, her word was absolute law.

Her first marriage was to my grandfather, a man named Gadd. They were both Londoners who had moved out to Oxfordshire between the wars. He was a singer – the nearest thing to a professional musician in family tree – who earned his living by travelling back to London and busking for West End theatre queues. I never met him, because years before I was born he'd left to live on the Isle of Wight. The official story was that he had TB and had gone there to live out his days, but there were very persistent rumours that he had another family there.

Gran had four children from that marriage. The eldest, Uncle Jim, spent most of his life in a lunatic asylum. Nobody in the family believed he was insane – they were convinced he just wanted to avoid working. He was fairly eccentric, though. He once took a job as a swimming pool lifeguard, but when after six months he actually had to save somebody he just ran round the pool screaming because he couldn't swim! After Jim in age was Auntie Ryne, my mother was next, and then came my Uncle John, definitely my grandmother's favourite and, through his guitar playing and singing, one of the biggest influences on my life.

John had joined the army during the war and was taken prisoner by the Japanese. He was put to work in a mine for six years, where the POWs were treated so badly that they ended up as skin and bone. After their release, there would have been an outcry in this country if they'd been brought home in that condition. It would have upset the peace treaties that had been signed and so, with very little publicity, the British government shunted them round the world for a couple of years to fatten them up – first to Australia, then on to the USA. He'd learnt to play the guitar from some Texans he was imprisoned with, and during his time in the southern states of America he'd become exposed to blues and country music and ended up a huge fan, of Hank Williams in particular. When he arrived home he had a large collection of records and could play with a real country blues feel. And country blues was the direct forefather of rock 'n' roll.

These styles were very new to Britain and completely unheard of in our part of the world at that time. In the late forties and very early fifties, all that was played on the radio was either live broadcasts of big band dances or songs from stage musicals. I was captivated by Uncle John's music. Although I was much too young to know what it was, I knew it was something completely removed from everything else. It had such rhythm and seemed to be much warmer and more soulful than the other music I was hearing then. I'm still Uncle John's biggest fan, and whenever I have a party I invite him to come along and sing.

Uncle John looks much like me. He's perhaps an inch taller and quite stocky, though not as prone to gaining weight as I am – he never put back on all that he lost as a POW – but facially we're very similar. He's craggy-looking, with a bigger nose and the same overlapping upper eyelids as me. And, like me, he has to fight not to squint. It's very much a Gadd look, as by all accounts my grandfather looked a lot like John and myself. My Mum has those facial characteristics, too. She's tiny, though, like my Gran, and she had very dark brown hair which seemed to turn absolutely white overnight when she was in her forties. She's nearly eighty now, and still very sprightly – all the Gadds were quick-witted and bossy but with a great sense of humour. I got a lot of that from them, especially in the way I like to be in charge of everything.

Before the war, after grandfather Gadd died, Gran married a man named Ewart Bodfish and moved the family from Sidford to Banbury. She had three daughters from that marriage – in order of age they were my aunts Mary, Pat and Jean. It was Pat who practically brought me up, as my mother was always working. She was only about twelve years older than me and more like a big sister; Pat used to drag us kids about with her, doing her best to keep us out of trouble.

In Banbury, my grandmother owned and ran a small bed-and-breakfast hotel with a tea room attached to it – 36 South Barr, the main road from London to Stratford-upon-Avon. That's where my mother came back to after Tony was born and we were given the attic room to live in while she worked in the family business. The tea room was a regular stop for coach parties, so it was always full of American tourists and Gran worried that my brother and I would irritate the customers. Making noise was the worst crime we could commit; if my grandmother ever thought she could hear any of us above the sounds of the restaurant we were sent straight up to our attic room for the rest of the day. But the real threat was to be put in the coal cellar. This only happened to me once, when I'd made too much noise going upstairs after I'd been sent up to our room for talking too loudly. I was in there several hours and it was terrifying – pitch-black, musty-smelling and with strange noises coming from the ceiling, which at that age I didn't realise was only people moving about in the room above.

My grandmother felt she had suffered in life and rather took it out on my mother for getting pregnant, which meant we had a tough upbringing. But my brothers and I weren't discriminated against within the family, and years later, when I talked to my uncles and aunts about this, it became apparent they had been treated in exactly the same way when they were kids. It was obviously just the Victorian attitude. At family mealtimes, for instance, we all used to have our meals sitting round one large table in the restaurant, after the main service, but there was never enough room for the children. We had to stand by the wall – *not* lean against it – until the adults had finished and left; only then could we sit down and eat. That wait was practically impossible to get through without doing something to upset my grandmother, which meant being sent up to the attic with no supper!

Gran also believed that children should make themselves useful, so I was constantly being sent out on errands. She liked to bet on the horses and enjoyed her tipple, but there were no betting shops in those days and bookies used to operate out of pubs. My most frequent task, therefore, was to go over to the Jolly Weavers. At the age of five or six I'd have to brave the thundering traffic on the main road we lived on to pass on her betting slips to the bookie or his runner (very clandestine, but everyone knew what was going on), then come back across that road carrying a jug of port and brandy. She would swear it was medicinal, and I believed her to such an extent that later in life I used to knock back the same mixture, convinced it was good for my throat!

But I don't want to give the wrong impression; my early days weren't all doom and gloom and hard work. In fact, I had quite a happy childhood. Growing up in the country at that time was an advantage – it meant we ate well and were probably healthier than city children. The land wasn't at all developed around there then, so my brother Tony and I would always be out playing in the fields or on farms. I was in the Cubs and played football for the Scouts, and there were always lots of Sunday school outings to the seaside and other towns.

There was a lot of love in my household, too. Mum didn't have much money, as we were living courtesy of my gran and all she got were her tips, but she always made sure we were well turned out. Canadian and American clothes used to get sent over to the nearby airbase, and as our tea rooms were popular with the American servicemen we'd end up with a lot of lumberjack-style shirts and jeans, which were considered a bit outrageous then. Mum always got us really good shoes – I can remember having my feet measured regularly. This was incredibly lucky because up until this day I've still got very good feet, which you need if you're going to make a career out of standing on stage!

My only real regret is that I never had any sense of immediate family. I had no father – Uncle John was my father figure – and my grandmother completely usurped my mother's role. Mum wasn't allowed to have the influence over us that a mother would usually have, because Gran always over-rode her. And as Gran was always so worried about us upsetting the customers, I used to feel as if we kids weren't that important. It wasn't that I felt unwanted – just that we only seemed to be there to get shoved out of the way.

There was always a lot of music at home. Because so many relatives lived either in the house or in the immediate area we had a lot of family get-togethers, when we would make our own music. The stars of those gatherings were my grandmother, who sang absolutely beautifully – when she finished 'I'll Take You Home Again, Kathleen' there wasn't a dry eye in the room – and, of course, my Uncle John, who was always being asked to get his guitar out and sing. The fact that Uncle John became the centre of attention when he sang left a very deep impression on me. By the time I was about seven he was playing rock 'n' roll and I was asking questions about music; then, a couple of years later, when my hands were big enough, he started teaching me chords and how to pick out tunes. But the earliest time I can remember his music having an effect on me was when I was two.

It was the first Christmas after Mum, Tony and I had moved back home, a time I'll never forget as I was recovering from an accident that could have changed my whole life; I bit my tongue off. I'd fallen down a long flight of stone steps outside Banbury Town Hall, and as I was rolling over I bit through my tongue, leaving it hanging on by a flap of skin. Fortunately, the St John Ambulance depot was in the same square and I was rushed to hospital. I got there, screaming and covered in blood, with Pat – who'd been with me – in hysterics and an ambulance man holding my tongue in my face, to be taken straight into the operating room where the surgeons were able to sew it back. My most vivid recollection of the accident was going under the gas just before the operation. The big overhead light seemed like stars bursting, and the sound of my breathing in the mask had this peculiar rhythm to it – *wheeeshi-lah-lah-lah*, *wheeeshi-lah-lah-lah*, *wheeeshi-lah-lah-lah*. After that, I had to leave my tongue hanging out for six weeks while it healed, which meant I couldn't talk beyond grunting and gasping and was only allowed fluids.

I was like this at the big family Christmas party, which at first seemed like the most wonderful event ever. It was one of the few times I can remember us kids having the run of the place and not being confined to the attic; fancy dress was mandatory, so everyone was in crazy costumes, and there was a huge spread of food with hundreds of little jellies. But it quickly began to go wrong for me. Firstly, I wasn't allowed any of the jelly I adored – I tried to blurt out '*Please* save me some!' but couldn't form the words. Then Uncle John, who was dressed as a cowboy, was called upon to sing. He had such a good voice that the room came to an instant standstill. Everybody crowded round him, women sat at his feet swaying along with the beat, and we all cheered for more. He clearly loved it, but I felt put out because up until then my accident had made *me* the centre of attention. When they moved away from me I felt like some freak stuck in the corner on his own, unable to speak and dribbling, while Uncle John became some sort of king.

I've never forgotten how miserable and embarrassed I was. And when I saw the reaction to Uncle John's singing I knew I wanted to be like him. I believe it was at that moment that I made up my mind to be a singer, because I can't ever remember wanting to do anything else.

A couple of years ago, the writer Roald Dahl's daughter Tessa asked me to contribute a story to a children's charity collection, so I wrote a piece about a young lad who desperately wanted some jelly but was unable to ask for it. I called the story 'Wishy La

La I Want Some Jelly'.

* * *

I went to a Catholic primary school. I was the only Protestant there, but as it was straight across the road from where we lived it was the most convenient place to send me. There I was, at six years old, marked as an outsider because of my religion. It came as quite a shock. I had to sit in another room during morning prayers, which upset me greatly because I loved the magnificent purple, gold and white robes the priests wore. They seemed to belong to a fantastic piece of theatre that I was excluded from – and for reasons I couldn't understand. Also, I quickly had to learn how to protect myself, because the other kids would pick on me constantly; firstly because I wasn't a Catholic, and secondly because I had no father. I had built up this image of a glamorous hero, but no one really believed it and I was always having to defend it.

The week I started school I was made milk monitor, and was very proud of it. When I started the job it was explained to me that it was most important to make sure everybody left at least an inch of milk in their bottle. Then I'd have to go and collect it from the whole school in a big white enamel jug. Once the jug was full I'd have to cross the road to Gran's guest house where I'd swap it for butter – in retrospect, I spent so much of my early childhood crossing that main road that I think I was quite lucky to have made it into my teens. It transpired that this private arrangement between my Gran and the school was the only reason I'd been given the honour. It wasn't because I'd earned it but because, in those days of rationing, Gran got extra butter stamps because she ran a tea room!

Another great anti-climax at school was discovering that not all women were pretty. Mum and her younger half-sisters were all young and attractive, and even my grandmother was still good-looking, so I'd really only been around pretty women. But at school there was a teacher who completely confused me. She was in charge of the milk and the butter, so I had to report to her every day, and she was hideous; built like a sack of potatoes, she had a moustache and always wore horrible lumpy stockings. Her disposition was thoroughly ugly, too. I was terrified of her, and although she was awful with the other kids she was worse to me because I wasn't a Catholic. One of my few fond memories is of a teacher called Sister Alison. She was always very kind to me, knowing that I didn't fit in. She was very good-looking, too, and I had my first serious crush on her.

All through that stage of my growing up I was obsessed with anything theatrical or showbizzy. Anything that was in any way larger than life I found totally fascinating, and for a small farming community Banbury offered a great deal that was exciting. It had the country's biggest cattle market – it was known as the Chicago of Britain – and every Thursday, market day, the pubs would open all day for the farmers, making the town seem the liveliest place imaginable to a seven-year-old. There was a strong sense of historical tradition, too. The nursery rhyme 'Ride a Cock Horse to Banbury Cross' was drummed into every child in the area, and there was an annual pageant in which a girl in costume and a long blonde wig rode a huge white horse through the town. That, to me, appeared the ultimate in glamour. We also had the annual Banbury Fair, which was held in the streets; the whole town was closed off for the day, 14 October. The highlight was a horse race from the top of the hill outside Banbury right through to the centre of town, and everyone used to turn out to watch it. It wasn't just events that influenced me, but people too. Even the Americans who were around the guest house all the time were to me, with my bumpkin accent, very theatrical. The loud, expansive 'Hi, how ya doin'? and the huge gestures were like nothing else that we had seen or heard. We kids would listen to them from upstairs and try to imitate them.

My only performing at that stage was in the annual Scout and Cub Gang Show – my speciality was to sing 'What Shall We Do with the Drunken Sailor' and dance the hornpipe – but I'm sure that everything I observed contributed to my approach twenty years later. From a very young age I figured it was more than just OK to show off – I was convinced it was actually a good idea.

I felt leader material quite early on. Because I was such an outsider at that first school, nobody would let me join their gang and I had to form my own. It was the same story after I left that school at the age of ten. We moved house so frequently that I was always changing schools and never had time to get in with the established playground cliques. Then, when I began getting involved in music, I was never just part of a group, I always set myself up as being slightly removed from the others – it had to be me *and* someone else: Paul Russell and the Rebels; Paul Raven and Boston International; Gary Glitter and the Glitterband. I've had to be in charge since I was about seven years old and joined the Cubs: I took over the six that I was put in, and was very quickly made sixer.

It really upset my cousin John, who had introduced me to the Cubs in the first place. He was the seconder of that six and had assumed he'd take it over, but I was promoted above him – not the last time my being bolshy would get me into trouble!

The other experience that made a huge impact on me during those years was going to London. It was unusual for children from my area to visit the capital – even a great many adults lived their whole lives in Banbury without ever venturing outside Oxfordshire – but I went twice before I was ten. The first time I was about four, and we kids were taken to the circus by a chap whom we called Uncle Stape, short for Stapleton. He was an ex-RAF flier and was around the tea room all the time as he went out with more than one of my aunts. He had what I thought was a vintage Rolls-Royce but have recently found out was a Bugatti, and one afternoon he packed me, my brothers and all my cousins into it and drove us up to Bertram Mills' Circus in Olympia. It was a wonderful event, with three rings going at once, and after the ride up there in that luxurious car I was left believing that London was the most exciting place on earth.

The next visit was two years later. I went to spend a weekend with Auntie Pat, now married and living with her new in-laws in Hounslow. We went all round the sights – Buckingham Palace, Trafalgar Square and Piccadilly Circus – and the scale and beauty of the old buildings reinforced everything I thought about London on my first visit. I knew that I had to go and live there.

I moved to London just before my twelfth birthday, by which time Mum was already living there and Tony and I had been in care for over a year. My mother had put us in a children's home in 1954 as it had become too difficult to look after us at the guest house. The business wasn't doing well, and Mum was practically running it single-handed. Aunt Pat couldn't help with us any more as she'd married and moved away, and Tony and I were like any healthy, growing boys – fighting, noisy and getting up to all the wild antics that lads of that age get up to. Gran, who was by then very old and drinking more and more, couldn't cope with us around the place any longer. Mum's plan was for us to go into the home while she found somewhere for us all to live – a temporary arrangement of only a few weeks. However, she hadn't realised that once children go into the care of the local authority it's very difficult to get them out, and Tony and I were in two different homes for a period of eighteen months.

The first home was in Wheatley, not far from Banbury. I wasn't too concerned, and for the first few days took it as a bit of an adventure. But when we went to a new school from there I knew something was wrong. I felt I'd been abandoned, and quickly became very unhappy. In what I now take to be a psychological reaction, I stopped eating vegetables and would only eat meat. But whatever I left on my plate would appear again at the next mealtime, and sometimes for up to five days in a row.

Unfortunately, I had no idea that such behaviour had a bearing on our chances of getting out of there quickly – as well as Mum proving that she could provide a stable environment to bring us up in, we also had to appear well balanced enough to live with her. It clearly worried her, though. She came to visit us almost every weekend and would bring with her a jar of Branston pickle and a bottle of tomato sauce. She'd smother my food with them and whisper, 'Just eat it up and let's get you out of here.' I used to run away from Wheatley regularly, as it was easy to get home to Banbury. That was partly why we were moved to another home, in Shillingford; it was thought that I wouldn't be able to work out the geography of the new area, so I wouldn't try to get home – and it worked. But also, as the move put us further from Banbury, it cut down my mother's frequent visits which the authorities believed were unsettling us. This was particularly hard on Tony: he was only eight and had always been spoilt at home, so he missed seeing Mum far more than I did.

We also had to go to yet another new school, and so, just as when we first went into care, we faced a tough time in two new environments. At school the other pupils teased us mercilessly because we were 'home kids'; while, back in the home, the other children used to resent us because we'd tell them it was a mistake our being there and we'd be going home soon. It was a defence mechanism, but it instantly set us apart, because a lot of the other children didn't have real homes to go back to and thought we were just being flash. It also meant we never even tried to fit in, as we'd convinced ourselves the arrangement wasn't permanent.

This second move left us more miserable than we'd been at Wheatley, but the worst aspect for me came in the autumn of 1955 when I started to enter puberty. I was worrying about my hair, getting spots and everything else that boys worry about at that time in life, and hated the fact that there was no privacy at all in the dormitories or washrooms. A particularly difficult situation arose when I started to notice girls. The kids at school made sure you were aware of the stigma attached to being in the children's home, so it was seriously embarrassing to admit to any girl that you lived in such a place. All in all I became very introverted while I was there.

It was during the summer of 1956 that Tony and I went back to Mum, who was by then living in Sutton on the southern edge of London. She had moved in with a man named Alan Prince Russell, and although they never married I took his surname, referred to him as my stepfather and called him Pops. He'd been something of a fixture in the tea room since about 1950, as he was a tour guide on the coach trips from London to Oxford and Stratford-upon-Avon, but I was never aware he was seeing my mother until Tony and I used to visit her at his flat in Brixton. The children's home at Shillingford would allow us to stay weekends there – separately, as Mum was only permitted limited access. We thought he was the most exciting person we'd ever met, not least because his flat had a swimming pool in the courtyard. He'd been a major in the army, and was very much a dashing, Douglas Fairbanks-style character – his nickname was 'Prang', as he was always crashing cars and coaches.

Pops was born in Durban, South Africa, to British parents, and went to Cambridge, after which he became dissatisfied with the regime in South Africa and moved to Argentina. He served in the army for twenty-one years and by the time he retired, just after the war, he'd travelled all over the world and learnt to speak fluent Spanish, Portuguese, Russian and Italian. Pops had a worldliness that really made an impact on Tony and me, and it was his spicy cooking – curries and chilli – that gave me the taste for exotic food.

Pops was instrumental in getting us out of the home. He'd noticed we weren't around the guest house any more, and when he was told why he invited Mum to go and live with him in London, promising to get a bigger house so that Tony and I could come there too. In order to satisfy the authorities he moved from the flat in Brixton before we were allowed out of care, and the two of us were seriously disappointed when we went to live in a very normal suburban house in Sutton West. But the relief at being out of the children's home more than made up for that, and, in fact, we were only there for a few months as we were constantly on the move during the three years I lived with Pops. I had more addresses then than I could remember, for although he had a well-paid job he gambled on the horses all the time – we were either rolling in money and living in absolute luxury, or completely broke and having to get out because we owed rent.

Practically every move meant a change in schools, so my education was by now a lost cause. We'd arrive at schools in mid-term, and be put in the lowest stream while they worked out what to do with us. These were the classes full of dunces and teddy boys, who were so disruptive that the only thing anybody learned was how to fight. Also, I was finding plenty of distraction as rock 'n' roll became huge in Britain. By 1957, when I turned thirteen, Elvis, Bill Haley, Gene Vincent and Tommy Steele were all being played on the radio and their records were on juke boxes in every café. I was obsessed.

2
Up West

In 1957 I got my first guitar. It was an old, very
ordinary, acoustic model and I started practising the
chords Uncle John had taught me. But I really wanted
to be a singer – I was the typical boy posing in front
of the bedroom mirror with my collar turned up,
trying to sneer like Elvis. By then I was going up to
the West End nearly every evening, getting the train
after school to meet Pops, whose coach firm was
based near the Houses of Parliament. He'd spend
every evening in the Silver Cross pub at the top of
Whitehall, where I'd sit on the stairs outside for a
while and then go and wander round Soho. I simply
couldn't see any point in sitting at home in Croydon,
where we were now living, when I'd read so much in
the music papers about a British rock 'n' roll scene
establishing itself in that area.

Naturally I ended up at the Two I's coffee bar,
which was *the* place to be. To me, aged thirteen, it
was like entering a different world. As you went down
the stairs into the club you were hit by a wave of heat
and sound and smells – it was like walking into a solid
wall of excitement. There were always at least two

19

hundred people packed into a space that would have been crowded with fifty in it. Everybody was streaming with sweat, and the noise was deafening. But that was everything I imagined rock 'n' roll should be. The kids may only have been wearing the clothes they went to work in, but the girls looked so glamorous. The acts that went on may not have been brilliant, but I saw them all as stars just because they were up on stage singing – and I could hardly believe I was standing just feet away from them. There were genuine stars down there, too: Cliff Richard was too famous by then, but Bruce Welch, Hank Marvin and Jet Harris were still regulars – this was before they renamed themselves the Shadows, and their act was called Cliff Richard and the Drifters.

One band that played frequently was Vince Taylor and the Playboys, who I still believe to be the best rock 'n' roll act I've ever seen. Vince was actually quite an awful singer, but his presentation was fantastic. He was about the only one to have his own band and they were the first to wear leather, even before Elvis. It was ridiculous, considering the heat down there, but it got them noticed. Vince's hair was dyed black while the rest of the group had bleached theirs peroxide blonde, and he took his mean and moody act to such lengths that off-stage he'd make out he was American, when in fact he was from Coventry. To him, a rock 'n' roller's image was everything, and he believed you shouldn't let the public see you as your real self, because you'd never appear special to them again. Much later that became one of my golden rules.

When I went back to the pub to meet Pops and get the last train back to Croydon, all I could think about was becoming a part of the rock 'n' roll world.

I knew I'd have to work to set myself up – I *had* to get the right clothes and the right guitar – so I got a series of jobs. I had a paper round in the morning, then sold evening papers outside a local factory after school; I was only thirteen and yelling 'Star, News and Stan-*daaard*' like a seasoned fairground barker. I went through Croydon market on Saturday afternoons selling the classified editions – the ones with the football results in – but the best job I had was a runner from the newspaper delivery van on Saturday lunchtimes. It was a job that gave me plenty of scope to show off – the driver would be on such a tight schedule that he'd just slow down at the drops and I'd jump out of the sliding door, drop off a bundle of papers, get back to the van and jump back in while it was still moving. My timing had to be spot on, because if I missed it I had to sprint to catch it up at the next set of traffic lights. The whole process was very flashy, and while the neighbourhood kids would look up to runners, they were always ready to give you a hard time if you missed the van! I'm sure that it was because of that training that my stage timing was always so good.

I was saving up for a guitar in the window of a local music shop – a red Hofner Senator, with a beautiful cutaway body and a scratch plate. The ultimate in cool, I'd fall asleep every night thinking about either Brigitte Bardot or that guitar! I was too young to get a hire purchase deal, so each day I'd give the shopkeeper everything I made from selling the papers on the understanding he kept the guitar for me. Of course this was taking ages, and eventually the old bastard sold it – it broke my heart. I was so cut up that I can't remember if he gave me my money back, but from then on I decided to concentrate on being a singer and not worry any more about guitars.

After I'd turned fourteen I started nagging Tom Littlewood, who ran the Two I's, to let me sing. That was the way singers got their start there – they pestered Tom until he gave them a chance. Usually there'd be one band on all evening, backing everybody; the pool of material was so limited then that every player knew all the songs – the singer would tell them what he wanted to do and just get on with it, hoping they played in the same key he sang in!

Everybody did three numbers, then Tom would flick the lights on and off, you'd stand outside on the fire escape for ten minutes to cool down, and on the way out Tom would pay you from the huge wad of notes he always carried.

The only real problem came if you were waiting to go on and the singer who was already up there was performing the same songs you wanted to do. So you had to have a couple of second choices ready, because it was important to avoid comparisons – it was bad enough that every singer looked the same, because they all had their collars turned up and in the dim lighting their faces couldn't be seen properly!

I sang a few times down there – Elvis and Buddy Holly songs – and I went down well enough to be asked to sing at another club in Soho. It was called the Laconda and was fronted by Diana Dors and a body-builder boyfriend of hers, but it was owned by the Kray brothers and was really just a drinking den for them and their cronies. While I was on stage, a crowd of frightening-looking characters would be sitting about getting legless. They'd make me sing soppy songs like 'Teenager in Love', which I didn't really care for, but they paid me very well.

I'd also do the occasional singing spot at the Latin Quarter, a well-established West End night club, but again what was required wasn't the rock 'n' roll I wanted to sing. And so, during 1958, I got my first group together.

There was a local Croydon lad called Mick on guitar and my best friend from school, Trevor Dry, on drums – or rather on a set of different-sized boxes, which he used until we got my stepfather to sign an HP agreement to get him some real drums – and together we'd practise Elvis and Buddy Holly covers and dream about making it big.

Later in the year, one of my stepfather's acquaintances in the Silver Cross opened a nightclub called the Safari Club in the same building as the Overseas Visitors' Club, just off Trafalgar Square. At first they put on established cabaret performers like Eve Boswell and Lita Rosa; then they decided they wanted to include rock 'n' roll, so Pops offered my services.

They were keen to use me, but I had to have my own group as the house band didn't know where to start. Initially my group back in Croydon weren't good enough, but at the beginning of 1959 the band leader at the Latin Quarter, Mr Raynor, introduced me to his son Pete who was an excellent guitarist. He lived near me in Norwood and could play all the Buddy Holly licks as well as do a bit of Bo Diddly-style finger-picking. Most important of all, he had a really good-looking red and black Burns guitar. So he joined the group, and together with Mick and Trevor on his new drums we became Paul Russell and the Rebels. We played the Safari from ten to half past eleven nearly every night, after which they rushed off to get the midnight train back to Croydon while I hung about waiting for my stepfather. We'd usually get home on the five o'clock milk train.

I'd stopped my morning paper round by now, but before I went up the West End in the evening I still had my pitch outside the factory. Often, though, I'd pay another kid to do it for me so I could get something to eat and play the juke box in the café. I'd go to the Two I's by myself at about eight o'clock, then meet the group and play the Safari, which soon started getting a very good crowd – I can remember dancing with Eartha Kitt and Connie Francis. Sometimes during the week I'd go on to the Latin Quarter afterwards, and on weekends I'd sing at the Laconda for the Krays and their crowd.

I was only fourteen and still going to school, where I slept through most of the day. The teachers didn't seem to care – they'd just put me at a desk at the back and leave me alone. I hadn't really settled enough at any school to realise I was missing out on anything – I don't think I ever properly found out what school had to offer. I honestly believed that doing the papers in Croydon market was all the education I needed; I lived by my wits, my sense of humour and my trustworthiness.

Of course, everything I was doing didn't leave much time for a normal family life. But that didn't bother me, because from as far back as I can remember I'd had such an odd home life that I didn't know how normal families lived. I'd always felt like a loner and never really knew what I was missing out on. The only time I've regretted this was when my son Paul was growing up and I started seeing a lot of him; I had no guidelines for how to behave towards him, so I'd ask him to tell me what he expected from a father and I'd try to act accordingly.

I was never around enough to find out how my mother felt about my activities, but I knew she didn't worry too much about me going up to the West End because I was meeting Pops, although I'm sure she didn't know I was wandering around Soho by myself at thirteen! Tony was always at home with her while I was out, which meant a lot to her as he was always her favourite. He was quietly becoming as obsessed with music as I was, but didn't get into it with me because of the age gap – the difference between eleven and fourteen is huge – and he was never as adventurous as me.

Mum certainly didn't try to stop me because, due to Pops' habit of playing the horses, the money I was bringing in – over £100 per week in 1959 – often proved useful. She didn't question where it was coming from, as she knew I was getting into the entertainment business. She knew I was doing well, too, because she'd come up to the Safari Club to have a drink with Pops every so often and see us play. Then by the age of fifteen I not only brought home a record with my name on it but had appeared on television singing. But in spite of that and all the cash, she never encouraged me. When I was singing around the house she'd tell me to 'Stop that row', and was always remarking how she didn't know why people paid to hear it. I never knew if she was joking or not, which could be a bit disconcerting. But I do believe she was very proud of me and simply taking the approach that most mums tend to follow – 'I'm not going to say too much to encourage you in case you get big-headed.'

Part of her attitude, I'm sure, was due to her being unable to come to terms with what was a very new style of music. She thought of it as a fad, and still hasn't quite realised that pop music is a saleable commodity and a respectable living to be in. She and my half-brother David, who lives with her now, are still astonished at my longevity. So is Tony, who went on to get a job in the music publishing department of Immediate Records in the sixties, and became a very accomplished guitarist. He still plays and sings in pubs and small clubs, and is a real rock 'n' roll purist – his collection of original records is fantastic and he knows every little detail about all of them: he'd probably be able to tell you what colour underpants the producer was wearing at the session! He used to think what I was doing in the seventies was nothing but a bastard-ised form of the music he loved, predicting that nobody would be interested for very long, and he still finds it very difficult to own up to liking any of it. Tony is an excellent musician, but he got married and settled down with a family before he ever had the chance to make it. He maintains he never wanted what I achieved, but I think he did want to succeed at playing music. He just never understood that having the talent – which he has got – is only a very small part of anybody's success story. He never had the blinkered, single-minded drive to be a star that I had from the age of thirteen.

Early in 1959 Paul Russell and the Rebels played at Hillingdon Youth Club, my first gig on the road – or, more accurately, 'on the tube', because we were all too young to drive. Carrying the guitars and drum kit in the rush hour, we took the train from Croydon to

26

Victoria, then the underground from there to Hillingdon, one stop from the end of the line. We were absolutely exhausted when we got there, but it didn't matter. When we arrived we were treated like stars, we played to a crowd practically our own age who went mad for us, *and* I got laid after the show. The ladies who ran the youth club each put one of us up, and where I was staying the daughter, an 'older woman' of about seventeen, climbed into bed with me. This was exactly the way I thought it should be, and it rekindled my enthusiasm for the music scene. Although we were earning good money in the West End, it was if we were the house band at the clubs we played in – almost a cabaret turn. The excitement was waning, and I expected so much more from it than that. But playing that gig at Hillingdon put the spark back and decided matters for me – I *had* to be a full-time rock 'n' roller.

A week after my fifteenth birthday I left school and home, and went to live in a bedsit in Clapham. I only went there to sleep and I saw the move as important to the rock 'n' roll lifestyle, which by now called for somewhere I could take girls back to. Mum and Pops didn't object to either development, but they persuaded me to get a 'proper job' so I could get a National Insurance card. I took the only regular employment I've ever had, working as an office boy for Ashton Mitchell, a theatre ticket agency. I spent most of my time trying to chat up the receptionist, and at the end of the first week I was paid £5. I never went back – it didn't make sense when I could bring in twenty times that amount from music.

From then on, rock 'n' roll was no longer a hobby – I was a professional. In spite of already earning so much money from it, I felt as if I was taking a huge step. I was scared, but I can also remember feeling totally exhilarated at the thought of the stardom I was certain lay in front of me. I felt like a racehorse in the stalls, raring to go but jittery with nerves. What made me cocky enough to imagine it would be easy was that I thought I'd already served my apprenticeship. But the next five years were to be one long, learning experience.

3
An Apprenticeship

By 1959 rock 'n' roll was accepted by the public, but the promoters and booking agents saw it as flakey, very much a fad, and hadn't explored its business potential. They were reluctant to move away from the old variety show formats in theatres that had had their heyday during the vaudeville years, and their only concession would be to put a singer on the bottom of a bill, announcing them as 'So and so, rock 'n' roll singer', as if they had a disease. So a few sharp characters moved in to cater for the demand. Rock 'n' roll virtually became controlled by a clique of gay Jewish entrepreneurs, of whom Larry Parnes was the biggest name. He had launched Tommy Steele three years previously and was the first to put purely rock packages in the larger theatres. Parnes's roster of clients included Marty Wilde and the Wildcats, Billy Fury and Tommy Steele's brother Colin Hicks. If a singer had talent and ambition, then a spot on one of Parnes's tours was almost guaranteed to make him a star.

That year was an excellent time to get into recording, too, as home-grown rock 'n' roll was well respected by the audiences but few acts were making records. Cliff and the Shadows were market leaders (they changed their name towards the end of the year); Marty Wilde was regularly in the Top 10; Billy Fury had two hits that year; Adam Faith came through with 'What Do You Want' in November; and Craig Douglas – a milkman from the Isle of Wight – began his brief run of hits from that summer. By then Tommy Steele had reinvented himself as an all-round entertainer, and Johnny Kidd and the Pirates didn't have any chart success until mid-1960, so the field was very open. Recording was a logical progression for me, but it was impossible to get through the door of a record company without a manager – you wouldn't be taken seriously. Larry Parnes would have been the obvious choice, but I'd heard too many rumours that you had to bend over as part of the deal. I don't know if they were true, but I was only fifteen and it scared me enough to stay clear. As this was just before Joe Meek's time the only other successful manager was an old variety agent called George Canjou. I approached him once, but as he already had one rock 'n' roller – Cliff Richard – he wasn't interested.

I became obsessed in 1959 with the idea of getting a manager and was taken on just before Christmas by Robert Hartford Davis, a Safari Club regular to whom I had been introduced by my stepfather. He was a small-time film producer and he seemed to have a lot of money. Although he knew nothing about music, he had a partnership with Mike Winters putting together variety shows, and had made a few music business contacts that way. He seemed to see me as an opportunity to make a name for himself as another Larry Parnes – as rock 'n' roll took off, an increasing number of small-time managers appeared in the clubs looking for unknown kids whom they could turn into stars.

Hartford Davis's first move was to take me for a meeting at the music publishers Campbell and Connelly in Denmark Street, to select some songs to record. I was *seriously* impressed by the idea. Not only was Denmark Street London's Tin Pan Alley and the absolute hub of the music business, but I was going to make a record and be given a choice of material! I felt as if I'd really made it, and so felt very let down when I was shown into a shabby little office and played a selection of drippy, ballad-type songs, none of which remotely suited me. And as it turned out I didn't have much choice in the matter – I was given a song called 'Alone in the Night', and didn't object because I was desperate to get my name on a record.

The session was at Decca, using its orchestra and backing singers instead of my group. We were given two hours to finish both sides. I didn't enjoy it too much, but at least I learned about different keys – previously I had known nothing about all this, and kept missing the change in the middle. I also discovered what hard work recording was: in those days it was done on single track, so if anybody made a mistake we'd have to go back to the beginning and start again. On about the 85th take the producer said, 'Oooh – that's a good 'un. We'll use that!' It all came as quite a shock to me, because I'd assumed that making a record was the result of careful crafting and aiming for perfection.

The record came out in January 1960 and wasn't a hit, in spite of me having changed my name from Paul

Russell to Paul Raven, which I thought was much more in character for a rock 'n' roll singer. It got me my next TV appearance, though, on *Cool for Cats* – one of TV's first pop shows. It featured artists singing their songs and a dance troupe which did contemporary routines to current hit records; in retrospect, it was an early prototype for *Top of the Pops*. The programme was presented by Kent Walton, before he became a wrestling commentator; Una Stubbs was one of the resident dancers.

After that I went back to working with the Rebels. As well as the Safari Club, Tom Littlewood had fixed us up with a Wednesday night residency at the Lyceum, and we were doing quite a lot of work at surburban youth clubs. In February, Hartford Davis and Mike Winters put us on a variety tour headlined by Bernard Bresslaw and with a very odd bill: Anthony Newley; an Italian tenor called Tony Dali who'd eat four bags of fish and chips and drink three bottles of red wine before he went on stage; Cherry Waynor, who was vaguely rock 'n' roll as she played the organ on *Oh Boy*; Mike Preston, who had just had a hit with 'Mr Blue'; and Paul Russell and the Rebels – they wouldn't call me Raven! – as the opening act. It lasted just over a week and was enough to convince the Rebels not to turn professional: the group split up as soon as we got back. I soon lost contact with them as I no longer lived in Croydon, but I heard later that Pete Raynor had joined the RAF and been killed in a rifle accident – a terrible waste of a brilliant budding guitarist.

Hartford Davis continued to manage me as a solo act, but we were falling out. I had not been paid for the Bernard Bresslaw tour as he told me the tour had made a loss; and after the unspectacular attempt at making a record with me he started losing interest. I think he felt he was the clever one of the operation and that he'd soon find somebody else to make him his fortune – in fact he was very fond of telling me that he could turn anybody into a star providing they were reasonably good-looking.

By April I was managerless and concentrating on live work again. I was immediately taken on by Hymie Zahl, a representative of Fosters Talent, a well-known theatrical agency that also handled MOR (Middle of the Road) acts like Johnny Mathis and Eartha Kitt. I'd met him through Hartford Davis and he seemed confident he could get me bookings. Hymie was gay, but almost blind, too, so when he came at you with his lips puckered and his arms out he'd never be quite sure where you were and you could easily duck. I remember him looking at my picture upside down and cooing, 'Pretty boy!' He was like Mr Magoo. Hymie booked me on a variety tour he was organising, which needed another rock 'n' roller on the bill. The show was to play Monday to Saturday in each theatre and then we'd spend Sunday travelling – an arrangement that was standard practice from vaudeville days; rather unwisely, these were called Week Tours. I wasn't keen to do it at first, but when I heard that Vince Taylor and the Playboys were on the bill I knew I could learn something. As it turned out, that tour certainly proved to be an experience.

We opened in Sunderland, and as soon as I arrived I had to go and rehearse with the show's orchestra. As we went through my songs the conductor would keep turning to me, rubbing his groin and mouthing at me, 'Oh, I do fancy you.' He was like one of Dick Emery's characters, and I was petrified! I thought I'd be safe when I got to my dressing room, but that was worse. I was sharing with the opening act, a sand dancer who had taken over the whole room. He'd been a pro for forty years and had acquired everything he needed for life on the road: the twenty-five feet of countertop was completely covered with boxes of make-up; he was using the whole clothes rail; he had an ironing board, a Primus stove and a kettle; and to save spending out on digs he slept there on a camp bed! He cleared a tiny space in front of a mirror for me, and then grunted at it. But I was so glad to get away from that conductor that I didn't complain.

As I was getting changed I started to whistle, probably because of my nerves. Without warning the sand dancer flew at me and his hands, with fingernails about an inch long, shot out at my throat. He was shrieking, 'You bastard, you bastard! Don't you ever do that in here! Get out, get out!' I was frozen with fear, and had no idea what I'd done until he shouted, 'You whistled! Never *ever* do that in a dressing room!' Finally he calmed down enough to tell me to go outside, turn round three times, swear as many words as I could think of, knock and wait to be asked back in. This I did, but it was too late: he told me I'd jinxed the show and that if it closed it would be entirely my fault. And it did close – that night. There were only about ten people in the audience, and the deal with each theatre manager was that if the house was less than half full on Monday they could cancel the rest of the week. According to the sand dancer it was all due to me, so when the acts were called together to be told the show was off, he pointed one of his talons at me and screeched, 'It was him! He closed the show! He whistled!'

I'm sure nobody took him seriously, but back then I wasn't to know. We were stuck in the same digs for a week waiting to move on to the next place, and I kept away from everyone as I was convinced that they were blaming me.

The effect of this incident has stuck with me so strongly that right to this day I won't have any whistling backstage. It's written into contracts. If people work for me and I hear them whistle they have to get out, turn round, swear, knock on the door and wait to be asked to come back in. Technicians and support bands think I'm a lunatic – I've heard them muttering, 'He can't do this to me – I'm in the union!' And of course in my heavy drug-taking days I'd imagine I could hear whistling all over the place and become quite paranoid with the idea that people were doing it just to get at me!

The tour lasted six weeks, during which I learned one valuable lesson from Vince Taylor – what to do if a husband comes home unexpectedly! We had gone off with two women after a show, and were in bed when we heard a key in the door. I panicked completely, but Vince, who'd been in this situation before, took charge and virtually threw me out of the nearest window. The girls flung our clothes out after us but we were too scared to get them, so quick-thinking Vince stole some sheets off a washing line and we walked back to our digs wrapped in togas and shouting, 'Hail Caesar!'

Back in London I returned to the Two I's, which was still the centre of the UK scene and useful because Tom would organise jobs for singers at small venues within easy reach of London – I'd do gigs at places like Chippenham Town Hall in Wiltshire or Colchester Corn Exchange in Essex. The local backing band would meet me off the train just before showtime, and I'd have to tell them what songs I wanted to sing on the way to the hall. Then I'd get changed and go straight on stage – nobody even knew what a sound check was! Whatever the group's real name was we'd usually go on as Paul Raven and the Twilights.

At the same time I was working regularly with two groups. One was the Ricky Allen Trio from Newport, South Wales, whom I'd met when they played the Two I's. They were always fighting among themselves – about any little thing – and needed a poseur like me up front to stop the audience noticing their black eyes and bruised faces. The other was the Vibratones, who were based in Essex. We did shows out to the east of London and I'd stay at the guitarist's mum's house if it was too late for me to get back to Clapham.

I was also going further afield than this with Roy Tempest, a specialist rock 'n' roll agent/manager, who had practically every village hall and a few larger town halls in the country sewn up with a network of local promoters. He'd book me to go to an area for a couple of weeks at a time and perform a series of one-night stands with either the local group or one which he'd sent along with me as a backing band. This arrangement lasted nearly a year and most of it was fun, but it was still nearly always tiny halls or youth clubs and I was only being paid peanuts.

In fact I was going broke, so in early 1961 I did another variety tour. It paid very well, and gave me my first chance to work abroad. Hymie Zahl had passed me on to the De Rouffanac Agency, where I was looked after by Vic Billings who later became my manager. He was sending a Southampton group, the Strangers, for a brief tour in Norway and they needed a singer, but one who had been played on Radio Luxembourg as that was the station which provided Scandinavia's rock 'n' roll. Because I'd had a record out, I fitted the requirement. I was billed as Paul Raven, Luxembourg Recording Star, and went down to Southampton to rehearse.

Later Vic phoned to say the Norwegian promoter insisted on the group having a black girl singer too, and that he was sending one down. There weren't many girl rock 'n' rollers about at that time, let alone black girls, so we had no idea what to expect. Shireen turned out to be Indian, a model and stunning-looking – but she couldn't sing a note. I rang Vic to tell him, but all he said was, 'Teach her, or you'll lose the gig.' We tried everything to get her to follow a tune without sounding flat, then realised our best hope was to play up her sultriness. We had her virtually talking the vocals – it was very moody. One of the guys sang high to add some tune, and I'd try to cover up as much as possible by singing *shoo be doo dum dums* in the background. When we arrived in Norway the promoter took one look at Shireen and whisked her away – after that, we only saw her once on the whole tour. It finally dawned on us that she had been part of the deal with Vic – he had to send a black girl out with us because the man in Norway fancied them! We'd sweated for a week to turn her into what could pass for a singer, only for her to be taken out to dinner, off skiing and then back to a posh hotel by some middle-aged promoter! I'm sure Shireen was just as much in the dark about the plan as we were, and it opened my eyes to the ruthlessness of the music business.

That trip taught me a lot, not least something I should have remembered in the seventies – don't trust anybody to do anything for you if it's worth more to you than to them. Before we went out, Vic had arranged with the promoter for glossy black and white pictures of me to be sold at the shows; I was to bring the money back with me. I'm not sure if it was part of the Radio Luxembourg Recording Star scam, or Vic's bonus for sending Shireen out. Anyway, before we set off I'd had my first-ever photo session, with Starpic; they were the top celebrity studios – Terry Dean, Marty Wilde and Cliff Richard were all photographed by them. I was given four huge crates of prints to lug from England – a burden which was constantly making us late for trains as the others wouldn't help me carry them. When we finally arrived, the promoter took one look at them and denied all knowledge of the deal. I didn't want to transport the pictures all the way home and I was also worried about what Vic would say, so I decided to sell them myself. I figured it wouldn't be so different from selling papers, so I went along the queues of kids waiting to come in; but, naturally, I didn't sell many before the show because nobody knew who I was. But when I came out to do our spot, the audience would recognise me and burst out laughing. Not being the last act on the bill, I had plenty of time to make sure I was outside with the pictures when the audience came out. Then I sold hundreds. Remarkably, one of those pictures turned up thirty years later on the set of *A Slice of Saturday Night:* the set dresser had found one and put it on the wall of the club next to a photo of Elvis.

Something I learned from the Strangers was how to get free accommodation. I couldn't understand why they didn't book into a hotel in each new town, so they showed me their dodge: after the show, when the girls came to the stage door for autographs, they'd appear worried and ask, 'Do any of you know where we can stay? We arrived so late our hotel had given our rooms away.' Often the girls would end up fighting over who was going to put which one of us up! That tour turned out to be like the Viking invasion in reverse – real rape and pillage time! The irony was that, as I was only sixteen, a condition of my work permit was that I phoned the British Consulate every night to tell them I was all right – they called it 'concern for my moral welfare'. Usually I made that call from the bed of a Norwegian girl, who, even as I spoke, would be doing her best to corrupt me!

Although I was making a name for myself with continual live work, my career wasn't progressing. The problem was that so little of it was taking place in London, which is where you had to be if you wanted to get into recording. And I did – badly. I had no manager, either, so when I got back from Norway and Hartford Davis offered to take me on again I accepted, in spite of my earlier differences with him. I felt I had no choice, and assumed that if he'd got me a record once then he could do it again. He didn't get me into a recording studio, though – he got me a part in a film instead. It was a semi-documentary that he was producing about the British rock 'n' roll scene, and it was called *Stranger in the City*. I was filmed doing a lot of turned-up-collar posing in Soho, singing outside the Two I's and on stage at the Lyceum. It was a real low-budget B picture, and because all I wanted to do was make records I wasn't very interested – I don't even know if it was ever released. Hartford Davis couldn't understand my attitude; he thought he was giving me a big break, but if he'd known more about me he would have understood my obsession with music. We didn't continue to work together after that, so all I could do was pester the people I'd met in Denmark Street to let me record a song. But the answer was always the same: nobody had the right material. Because all the top acts would cover American hits, British songwriters weren't bothering with rock 'n' roll. It seemed a hopeless situation, so, when, in the summer of 1961, Vic Billings offered to manage me and said he could arrange a recording contract with Parlophone Records, part of EMI, I jumped at it.

My first session for the company was with a band who weren't going to follow a score. 'Working without dots', it was called, and it allowed the musicians to be spontaneous. It hadn't been attempted at EMI before, but given this freedom the six-piece band, led by Bill Shepherd who went on to arrange all the BeeGees' sixties' hits, excelled, and inspired me to give 200 per cent. It was more like a sweaty night club jam than a staid recording session and the record, a cover of the bluesy American number 'Walk On Boy' had a wonderful raw excitement to it. Because of the style of recording it got a lot of press coverage and I was on the front page of *Disc*, hailed as Britain's first R&B singer. It sold 25,000 copies within three weeks of release. I was never going to get rich from it as my deal gave me only a penny per record sold, and as there were 240 pennies in a pound that left about £100 to be split with Vic. But I was too excited to worry, because I knew I'd made a *good* record this time.

I was looking forward to having a hit when George Martin, the head of Parlophone, summoned me to his office and told me he wanted me to record a Bacharach and David song, 'Tower of Strength', which had been a US hit for Eugene McDaniels. Immediately! I wondered why, because this would mean withdrawing 'Walk On Boy' which looked certain to get into the Top 20. Obviously I couldn't have two singles floating about at the same time but I was in no position to argue. He explained he'd heard that somebody else in the UK was about to record the song, so he wanted to release it first. The session was fixed for the next day at Abbey Road, in a studio the size of a cathedral, in front of a full orchestra – timpani and everything. Coming straight from that highly successful free session I found the atmosphere a bit stifling, but it was such a great song that it was almost impossible to sing badly.

The record came out in November 1961, a week before the other version by Frankie Vaughan. My version got a better initial reaction – it was said mine was the more interesting voice – but just at the same time there was a TV strike which was broken only by *Sunday Night at the London Palladium*. Frankie Vaughan went on there four weeks running, singing 'Tower of Strength', and his record stayed at Number One all through December. I did eventually get to do *Thank Your Lucky Stars* with it, and Muriel Young's *Tuesday Rendezvous*, one of the kids' TV shows on which pop singers appeared, but by then it was too late.

Parlophone dropped me after that, and it became impossible for Vic to interest anybody else. Because I'd been at the two biggest companies and not got anywhere, the others assumed I was never going to make it. For the next eighteen months I did odd bits of session singing and tried to fall back on live work, but it was nowhere near as lucrative as the previous three years. I was working for Roy Tempest again, mostly with a group called Johnny Milton and the Condors. We were paid £18 and petrol money per show and would go all over the country – Southend one night, Glasgow the next – doing three or four gigs a week.

I then entered a period in which I became so broke that at one point I was thrown out of my bedsit and taken in by the Jamaican family next door, who felt sorry for me. I could hardly understand a word they said – the first time I had Sunday lunch with them I had to ask if they were speaking English – but they were so good to me I'd love to track them down now and thank them properly. Another virtual life-saver was a job that Vic fixed up, doing the voice-over for the Cherry B TV commercial – 'Cherry B, Cherry B, Cherry B, it's the sparkling drink for you and me!' Then what sounded like a little girl squealed 'It's Cherry B for me!' except in reality it was a fat old lady! It was hardly rock 'n' roll, but we'd take anything at that time.

Vic and I really struggled through the first half of 1963, too. Johnny Milton and the Condors had gone to Germany to work – a lot of groups went over after the Beatles came back – so I couldn't even go on the road with them. We were still surviving – just – on what money I could pick up doing occasional session singing, which wasn't very much. We were just on the point of starving when the Cherry B advert must have got another TV run, because out of the blue Vic received a cheque for £180 for it. He had to cash it in a local shop, because if he'd gone to the bank his overdraft would have swallowed it up. With our new-found wealth we treated ourselves to a huge Chinese meal in the West End and as soon as we'd finished eating we both rushed outside and threw up in the street – we hadn't eaten so much in one go for such a long time that our stomachs couldn't take it!

Then Vic started managing Dusty Springfield, who was about to go solo. While it immediately brought in some cash, it also led to the only career deviation I've ever been through, when I went to work in television. A friend of Dusty's, Vicky Wickham, was secretary to Francis Hitchins, the editor of a new pop show about to be launched called *Ready Steady Go*. It was because of Dusty that *Ready Steady Go* became what it was. The only music she ever played at home was the lighter side of American soul – Motown, Stax, Ike and Tina Turner and so on – and naturally this influenced Vicky, who was so closely involved with the show that it evolved into the UK showcase for all the emerging black American talent. These artists had hardly ever been seen in Britain, yet their music was played in clubs in major cities during the new Mod youth cult. As well as featuring this music, the show also wanted to break new ground by turning the crowd into stars. It was meant to be a cross between two US shows, *American Bandstand* and *Soul Train*, in which cameras would move around the whole studio and film the audience as well. The British TV establishment was sceptical, but as news of this innovation started leaking out there was an air of great expectancy among teenagers. This was going to be *their* show!

After the first two broadcasts, however, it was obvious that something was wrong. The studio audience wasn't nearly glamorous enough, so the atmosphere was flat. It was decided they needed to be more selective and not just invite any old viewer who wrote in for tickets – but no one knew how to go about it. Vic suggested that I should be the one who invited kids along: I knew the right clubs and could go and find them. So I became the programme assistant, and would go to Mod hangouts such as the Flamingo, the Scene and Crawdaddy's, giving out tickets to anyone who was dressed sharp, in all the Italian gear, and knew how to dance. We thought we'd got it right, but because part of the Mod pose was to act cool, once they were in front of the cameras they just stood around looking bored, like they were still in a club trying to impress each other. We wanted them to scream, so I became a warm-up man. I'd wind them up for about half an hour and rehearse their reactions to the acts, so that when the show went on air at least there was some excitement. I'd also take about a dozen of the best-looking ones into another studio and dance with them to make them lively, then position them where the cameras could pick them out for close-ups.

I quickly became part of the programme's team: Vicky, presenters Cathy McGowan and Michael Aldred, and myself would have meetings to decide who would go on the show. It was a situation that invited corruption – at the end of 1964 Donovan's manager, Geoff Stephens, was taking me out for Chinese meals nearly every lunchtime and nagging me to get Donovan on to the show. At first I didn't think he was right for us, but eventually I gave in and he was on for four consecutive shows. Straight afterwards he got a record deal. I got quite powerful in my capacity as the audience inviter, too. Just being on the show meant a lot to the kids. A select few – mostly picked by me – would be invited afterwards to the Green Room, a tiny hospitality suite. All the acts would be in there, so the kids were offered the chance to mingle with the likes of the Beatles, James Brown, the Stones and the Supremes – all their heroes. The party always continued at the Ad Lib night club, which was owned by the chap who later opened Tramp: any kids who played their cards right would get invited down there, too. A *Ready Steady Go* invite became the hottest ticket in town, and a lot of girls would do literally anything to get one – I could have had the time of my life.

After the shows Dusty would throw parties, too, which were always lively affairs. They were attended by the groups, the production team and a who's who of the London in-crowd. She would always lay on a magnificent spread, but at almost every one she'd end up throwing food about – she'd start with the buffet, then get stuff out of the kitchen. She did it because she was a little neurotic and a bit of a tomboy, with plenty of rock 'n' roll spirit. I vividly remember the first one I went to, when I was wearing the most wonderful, tailor-made mohair suit which ended up covered in flour. Dusty was short-sighted, too, so she'd often throw food over people who weren't prepared to enter into the spirit of it – several important music business executives have left her parties wearing the salad!

At the first party I went to, the Supremes and Martha and the Vandellas were there, and I was standing in the hall when Diana Ross came running out of a room screaming and begged me to take her back to her hotel. She was shaking, so I calmed her down a bit and asked what was wrong. Bones Ross, as we called her on *Ready Steady Go*, pointed into the party and shrieked, 'That woman! It's that woman! Every time I'm in the same room as her she jumps on me!' All the way back to her hotel I tried to find out who 'that woman' was, but she either didn't know or she just wasn't telling.

So *Ready Steady Go* opened up all sorts of possibilities in my social life, but by now I was deeply in love and about to get married. Ann, my future wife, worked in the London Palladium box office, and I had first met her at the Two I's when I was fifteen. At the time I fancied her desperately but couldn't get near her – I went out with both her best friends so I had an excuse to hang around her, but it didn't help my case when I went to bed with them! So nothing happened then, but Ann and I kept bumping into each other over the next couple of years. We called it 'forever getting in each other's way', which convinced me we were programmed into life's great computer, and made me fancy her even more. Then I didn't see her for over a year until we met in Brixton, where I was then living, in 1962. I invited her round for lunch the next day and rushed round the shops to buy some food. I had to lay on something impressive, so I spent my last few shillings on a packet of fish fingers and a bag of frozen peas. But they didn't even get cooked because the moment she stepped through the door we were at it like knives! From then on we were inseparable.

I had to move soon after that – I was always too broke to pay my rent – and went back to live in Clapham in a room in one of Vic's friends' flats, Michael Baldwin. He was a costume designer at Rediffusion TV and instead of charging me rent I had to model the designs he was working on. When the flat below became empty Ann rented it, but I didn't move in with her. She still spent 90 per cent of her time in my room, although when her parents visited she would run downstairs to pretend she was living a morally irreproachable life.

We got married in 1964, just before I turned twenty, and we're sure our son Paul was conceived on our wedding night, which is odd because we'd practically lived together for eighteen months and had never taken any precautions. In the beginning of our relationship I was at great pains to stay faithful when I was on the road, and likewise at *Ready Steady Go* – mostly because of Ann, partly because I took the job very seriously. But every week I was faced with some of the most beautiful girls in London begging me for tickets to the show. Since I was a weak-willed nineteen-year-old, it was only a matter of time before I yielded to temptation. Ann had a fair idea of what was going on, and after we were married she used to wag the finger at me about it. I'd storm off in a huff thinking I might as well be hung for a sheep as a lamb, and made sure I did even more than I was already being accused of. Then I'd come home feeling guilty, and that would make me irritable. It was a vicious circle that wasn't any of Ann's making, and she was never going to get the better of it.

Officially the marriage lasted three years, but in reality it wasn't nearly so long. When we were talking about marriage my fondness for Ann made me lose hold of the fact that I wasn't ready to settle down yet. I'd never known a regular family life and so didn't know what rules to play by. There was always so much going on outside the home as well that our relationship didn't have much of a chance. It completely fell apart when I went over to Germany in 1965 and worked there for four years. For a long time we'd be very passionate every time I came home – our other child, Sarah, who was born in 1968, was conceived during one of those visits – but as we'd spend weeks at a time away from each other we naturally drifted apart. I began a serious affair in Germany and Ann got involved with my best friend at home.

When I moved back to the UK I never did see much of our kids. My lifestyle made access very difficult – I was either on tour, living in a shabby bedsit or dossing on somebody's sofa – and it just didn't seem fair to wander in and out of their lives. It wasn't until I'd become Gary Glitter and bought my house in the country that I started seeing Paul regularly, because then he could come down and stay. He was about eight or nine years old before I got to know him, and it was even later than that before I formed any relationship with Sarah. Ann did a great job in bringing them up, but she felt very bitter towards me. I can't blame her, either – I would have felt the same. It's really very sad because for a few very happy years we cared for each other a great deal.

* * *

By the end of 1964 I was very bored at *Ready Steady Go*. Seeing the groups on there every week was a niggling reminder of what I'd set out to do myself. There was a boom in blues music at the time – Alex Korner, the Steampacket, John Mayall, Long John Baldry – but it was happening away from the mainstream pop scene in pubs and tiny clubs. Watching these hard-working, imaginative blues bands, after a year and a half of the almost unreal glamour of *Ready Steady Go*, it struck me how much more honest they were – much closer to what I believed to be the spirit of rock 'n' roll. There were a lot more bands than singers on the circuit, and as R&B was a style in which I'd already proved myself as a singer I started to get offered singing spots. I began working regularly with a South London soul and blues outfit called Anzaks. We never had any large-scale success – our biggest claim to fame is that David Essex was a huge fan and turned up at most of the gigs – so there was never any question of me giving up my well-paid day job at *Ready Steady Go*. But it had made me realise how much I'd been missing performing, and I knew that as soon as the right job came up I'd be back on the road – as I had a baby to support by then, secure employment was a major priority. It was then that Mike Leander made me what seemed like an offer I couldn't refuse.

In the seventies, as manager and producer/co-writer of all my hits, Mike was *the* major force in my career, but in 1965 he was just somebody I knew socially through *Ready Steady Go*. We couldn't have come from more different backgrounds: he was a former public schoolboy who had begun to work for a law degree, but was so obsessed with music that he had given it up to study orchestration and conducting at Trinity College of Music. His career got off to a flying start when he joined Decca Records as an A&R man/in-house producer, and after arranging the Rolling Stones' early recordings got promoted to musical director of the company at the age of twenty-two. In the entire UK record business, nobody that young had ever been put in such a responsible position. During the sixties he produced 'It's Only Make Believe' and 'Thoughts of You' for Billy Fury; worked in America with Burt Berns, as arranger for the Drifters and Ben E. King; did the string arrangement for 'She's Leaving Home' on the Beatles' *Sergeant Pepper* album; wrote the hit singles 'Lady Godiva' for Peter and Gordon, 'Early in the Morning' for Vanity Fare, 'I've Been a Bad Bad Boy' and 'High Time' for Paul Jones; and produced the first records of Joe Cocker (whom he signed to Decca as an unknown) and Van Morrison.

He used to come to *Ready Steady Go* with Marianne Faithfull, as he'd produced her cover of 'As Tears Go By' – he arranged the strings on the Stones' recording of it, too. Everybody was certain that Mike and Marianne's relationship was something more than professional. It seemed she was sailing very close to the wind, as she was getting married to John Dunbar about then, *and* it was obvious she was seeing Mick Jagger. At times it got a bit complicated, and there was always a lot of whispering in corners when Marianne was there.

Mike was aware of me as a singer, and when we went out for drinks he'd tell me I had one of the best R&B voices Britain had ever produced. He was always asking why I wasn't earning my living at it any more, and then one day he told me he was forming the Mike Leander Show Band, and asked me if I wanted to join. I wasn't keen to be part of a band – I'd always seen myself as an Elvis clone – until he explained the set-up. It was to be a nine-piece outfit, including a brass section, fronted by two singers – his writing partner Chas Mills was the other one – and we'd do Righteous Brothers-type harmonies. The sound Mike was looking for was a powerful, jazzy swing, like Chicago or Blood, Sweat and Tears did later. Blood, sweat and tears, however, is an apt description of what it was like for me in that band!

The group was booked from April to October 1965 for a thirty-week tour with the Bachelors, who'd been the second-biggest selling group of the previous year, behind the Beatles. The bill included Susan Maughan, Freddie 'Parrot Face' Davis and a troupe of dancing girls. It sounded too much like a seaside special for me, but I was told we'd be making records for Decca as well, so I jumped at it.

During the first week, in Gloucester, we brought the place down. The band was brilliant. On numbers like 'You've Lost That Loving Feeling' and 'Getting Mighty Crowded' the brass put real soul into it and the kids in the audience went mental. But we were on right before the Bachelors and either they or their management complained about having to follow us, so the billing was altered. The pit orchestra was sacked meaning the band had to back the whole show, which greatly reduced its impact, while Chas and me did a short spot midway through. Nobody was happy about it, the orchestra least of all, but we couldn't pull out without losing a lot of money: the band had turned down other work to make themselves available for thirty weeks, and I'd left *Ready Steady Go*. I complained louder than anyone else, though, which got me marked as a trouble-maker and demoted to opening the show with the dancing girls – joining in the routine and singing 'We're gonna dance, we're gonna dance! We're gonna live it up all night l-o-o-ong!' Diabolical stuff, but I had no choice other than to go with the flow. The only perk was sharing a dressing room with the girls – and sharing digs with a few of them. I spent a lot of time going to the betting shop for the Bachelors and pulling women for them – they'd send me out into the audience to chat up the girls they fancied and talk them into coming backstage!

Halfway through the run, while the show was playing in London, the promoters – Phillip and Dorothy Solomon – informed me the tour was to be extended by a week and asked if I was available. By then I'd had enough and told them no way, I'd rather starve. They didn't seem too bothered, but the next week, when we were in Newcastle, they sacked me, giving as the reason my refusal to do the extra week. It was sheer spite. They could easily have got rid of me in London, but they wanted to cause me as much bother as possible. On reflection, it was no more than I should have expected – they'd behaved despicably since day one of that tour. It seemed to me that they enjoyed wielding power and forcing their acts into positions where they could be treated with no respect and had to do maximum work. To this day, they are probably the only two people I genuinely wouldn't care what became of them.

Mike couldn't plead my case – he'd left the show after that first week, and as he was managed by the

Solomons he couldn't really have done anything. I don't believe he knew what was going on, anyway. All I could do was travel home to try and pick up what singing jobs I could. The band and I had recorded some obscure soul songs before the tour started, but they were never taken to the release stage so that avenue had come to an end. Then in November John Rossall, the Show Band's trombone player, rang me up and told me he'd got together with an Irish group called Boston International to go and work in Hamburg, but they needed a singer. As I'd stayed in contact with Johnny Milton, who'd told me about the almost limitless work for British groups in Germany, and as there was nothing happening for me in England, I'd been considering trying my luck over there. John's call made my mind up for me.

4
Teutonic Nights

We went to Germany as Paul Raven and Boston International (depending on how we wanted to present ourselves, we'd often change the group name to either the Boston International Show Band or the Bostons). Rock 'n' roll had been introduced to northern Germany by Radio Luxembourg, which had broadcast there since 1962, and a succession of UK bands going to work there had firmly established it. By 1965 practically every establishment that could hold more than fifty people and get a liquor licence had reinvented itself as a live music club; cinemas had taken their seats out and put in tables; bars put in stages; cellars had been cleared out to make dive bars; and long-standing cabaret clubs had renamed themselves as rock venues. The demand for British acts soon became such that it didn't matter how awful a band sounded as long as they were from the UK and had long hair. Bands from London, because of its 'swinging' reputation, enjoyed a higher status, so it was commonplace to meet groups with impenetrable Geordie or Birmingham accents passing themselves off to club owners as genuine cockneys.

Through a club manager who had come over to London to audition groups we'd been offered a three-month engagement at the Kaiserkeller in Hamburg; this was the first club the Beatles ever played in Germany – *not* the Star Club, as legend has it. After the bleak times I'd been experiencing since leaving *Ready Steady Go*, it seemed too good an opportunity to miss; plenty of women, plenty of booze and, most importantly, plenty of work. It was everything I'd looked forward to as a singer, but our arrival was more like a flashback from the Hillingdon Youth Club gig I'd done with the Rebels. Because we were too broke to get a van we'd travelled to Hamburg by train and ferry, carrying all our gear. We survived all right until we got to the city, where we had to take the U-Bahn, the underground, to the club. It was the middle of the rush hour and we had to hold the doors open to load and unload our instruments. The commuters were screaming: '*Raus! Raus!*' – 'Get out!' – at us, and as I listened to the guys in the band shouting 'Fuck off!' at them I stood back, dazed, and asked myself if I'd really made any progress over the last six years! To make matters worse, the chap who had hired us owned two clubs and we arrived at the wrong one.

We finally found the right one, where we had to play from seven in the evening until three in the morning; eight shows of forty minutes, with twenty minutes' break in between each. The first time we got on stage we looked out into the audience and could hardly believe the amount of seriously attractive women in the club – I'd never seen so many blondes in one place before. I could hardly wait for the break to find the girl I'd been eyeing up, but as we finished our set a cinema screen was winched up out of the floor, there was a complete blackout and they started to show a clip of *Jailhouse Rock*. Every break was the same: they'd screen twenty minutes of an old Elvis or James Dean movie, plunge the club into complete darkness and leave us to stumble about trying to find the girls we fancied! Too often I would have just groped my way to the right table when the twenty minutes were up, the lights would go on, the screen was cranked down into the stage and we'd be back on. Even if I did manage to find the girl's table in time, the language barrier made it practically impossible to chat her up in the dark.

Getting off with women was not only desirable but necessary, as it was the only way to ensure a comfortable night. Our agreement with the club specified that accommodation would be provided – and we were being charged against our wages for it – but all it turned out to be was a tiny room above the club with eight bunks and four cupboards in it, and the only facilities were the club's toilets. Two of the band, Tommy and Jimmy Murray, wore the same clothes for five years. To save money on meals we bought a Primus stove and cooked in there too, so the place smelled absolutely terrible! If I couldn't get to go home with a girl – and some of them got quite snotty when they discovered I was more interested in their bed and their bath than I was in them – I'd just go out and wander round the city. That's when I started buying the wake-you-up pills that dealers sold openly in the toilets at the club; Captigun or Preludin both worked as well as each other, but the latter tended to give me the runs. With a handful of pills and three bottles of brandy I could stay awake for a week. Quite often I did, because anything was better than going back to that room.

But I loved the performing side of that three-month engagement. We were already good when we went out there, but improved greatly for two reasons: firstly we had no musical director telling us what to do and so we were free to experiment with our arrangements; and secondly, competition from other bands was so intense that we knew the club owner wouldn't honour our agreement if he thought he could get better for the same money. The Bostons was a large band with a full brass section, so we could handle just about any musical style; we excelled at the soul music that was very popular, played cover versions of virtually anything that was in the Top 20, and threw in a bit of straight rock 'n' roll any time the proceedings needed livening up.

If my first six years had been an apprenticeship, Germany was my finishing school. I developed my stage act far beyond the Elvis/Eddie Cochran rip-off it had tended towards, and got to understand exactly how to read a crowd too, to give them exactly what they wanted. This was incredibly important, as we had to please three very distinct audiences. At weekends the club charged admission and attracted a more sophisticated crowd who didn't like their music too raw, so we'd play a lot of Motown covers. Admission was free during the week, and as soon as the place opened a very young crowd would come in – screamers who wanted anything energetic and plenty of current pop songs. They had to leave by nine-thirty, because in Germany at that time there was a curfew on kids under sixteen – they all carried ID cards and had to be off the streets by ten o'clock.

After the kids had gone the students would come

in, and they appreciated musicianship; for them we'd play mostly blues. However, the whole ambience of the club would change too, because a system known as *Umsatz* came into operation and customers could only remain as long as they had a drink in front of them. The university crowds would come in already drunk from the cheaper bars, buy one beer and sit nursing it while they watched the band. As the waiters were on commission they were never too happy about this, and I saw the most brutal occurrences; customers would get clouted round the head so they'd spill their drinks, or get beaten up if they didn't leave quickly enough; the very drunk would get blatantly robbed, their pockets gone through in full view of everyone. The owner was perfectly well aware of what was going on, but as he wanted to sell as many drinks as possible he would turn a blind eye. He was a part-time cat burglar as well, so the club was always being raided by the police looking for him in connection with local break-ins. All in all, the Kaiserkeller was a den of iniquity.

When we came to the end of our three months the owner said he wanted to keep us on, but an Englishman I knew from the Two I's made him an offer for us on behalf of another club. It was an open-ended arrangement at a night club in Kiel called the Star Palast, but I wasn't too keen on going. I'd been married nearly two years but had hardly seen my wife, and even though the band were excellent to work with I wasn't too happy with them off stage. They were all drunkards by then and the living arrangements were depressing me; one day the Murray brothers – the worst piss artists in the group – came in legless, broke into my wardrobe and ate all my food. When I arrived back they were still there, still drunk, with empty food wrappers lying all around them. I couldn't wait to get home. But the others were very young – eighteen or nineteen – and had no real reasons to go back; they just wanted to carry on working and enjoying themselves, so they talked me into staying.

The Star Palast offered exactly the same type of accommodation, but the first thing the club owner, Manfred Wotilla did, was to take our passports on the pretence of getting us fixed up with work permits. We didn't get them back for six months. I felt as if I was in prison, knowing I couldn't just take off if I wanted to. Because we didn't know the town either, and had no money, we spent most of our days hanging round our room. For entertainment we used to hold seances: we rigged up a ouija board and would sit around it calling up the ghosts of Buddy Holly and Eddie Cochran – we were so full of pills all the time we actually believed we reached them on a few occasions. Wotilla was always frantic to find out what we did in there all day – he could hear us laughing – so one day he went up on the roof to look in through the skylight. During this particular seance, just as the glass started moving – one of us usually got bored and pushed it – the light bulb above us exploded! We freaked. Completely. We screamed, some guys ran out of the room, some dived under the beds, and Wotilla fell through the skylight! It was mayhem in there for about a quarter of an hour, and we were banned from holding any more seances.

These moments were fun, but tensions between band members were starting to surface. Money was the main issue. John Rossall handled all the financial arrangements, and although we knew we were getting paid more in Kiel – we were doing twelve hours instead of the seven in Hamburg – we still had barely enough money to eat. Something was obviously going on. The Murrays weren't helping our financial situation either, because while we were working band members could go to a side bar where any drinks ordered would be marked off against our wages – the wages for the group as a whole. Tommy and Jimmy would go back and forth so often shouting, '*Noch ein Bier, bitte*', that we'd frequently finish the week owing the club money.

Matters came to a head when, after we'd been there nearly a year, Jimmy Murray saw John coming out of a post office when he was supposed to be somewhere else. Suspicious, he went through John's pockets and found deposit slips which showed that he'd been sending large sums of money back to England. When we all tackled John about it he started to cry. At first he said it was to support his Mum who was very ill, but eventually he told the truth. It turned out that he was in league with Wotilla and was allowed to skim money off our wages as a fee for keeping us there – if ever we threatened to leave it was John's job to talk us into staying.

We also found out that John was paying the drummer, Ronnie Brambles, more than the rest of us because – so he said – Ronnie was very good and difficult to replace. Not only did we feel that this was unfair, but it came as some surprise, because Ronnie was famous for pleading poverty. He'd never buy meals, but just sit down with us and start nagging, 'Do you want all those chips?' or, 'Are you gonna finish that sandwich?' so we'd feel sorry for him and feed him – he was only sixteen. So we turned on Ronnie, who assured us that he was using the money to pay for his drum kit – and we believed him. When we got home a couple of years later, though, he had a brand-new Mini Cooper waiting for him. Everybody was very curious as to where the money for that had come from.

John Rossall had been terrified when we challenged him, and I think he started playing it straight with the band after that. I was never quite sure, though, because I used the situation to opt out from his deal and organise my own payment and living arrangements. I did well out of that, too: Wotilla knew the audiences loved me, so he had a lot of respect for me. But negotiating pay rises with him was another matter. Apart from being quite a frightening individual – anybody who ran a night club in a tough sea port had to be – in his outer office he used to keep a parrot that would scream four words, in English, at anybody who came in: 'Money cut! Fuck off!' Just to intimidate visitors even further, Wotilla would leave them out there for ages before inviting them into his office. If you still had the courage to ask for more money, his reaction would be to roar with laughter and trot out some lame excuse.

On one occasion, pilled up to my eyebrows and spoiling for a fight, I told him if he didn't give me a rise I'd smash the pinball machines in the club one by one until he agreed. He just threw back his head and laughed. In a fury I stormed out, punched through the glass on one machine and cut my hand badly. I was moving on to attack the next one when the waiters burst in led by their unofficial head, Ziggy. Now Ziggy hated me because I'd had an affair with his girlfriend who worked behind the bar. Although I'd seen his notorious head butts in action practically every night during *Umsatz*, nothing could have prepared me for receiving one – I thought my head had exploded. With blood pouring down my face and from my cut hand I tried to hit him, missed completely and put my fist through a glass door. Then six waiters set upon me and gave me the hiding of my life, after which – at Wotilla's instruction – they took me to hospital to be stitched up. I was on stage that night, full of speed and painkillers and with my hand in a sling. And I got my rise.

I lived in Kiel for four years, and for the first two lost contact with Britain altogether. I knew much more about what was happening in America, because there were always a lot of US sailors in town who'd sell us soul records and teach us the dances. The band changed line-up frequently, although John, the Murrays and Ronnie Brambles were always there. We built up quite a following in the city and I became quite Germanised too. I soon had a basic command of the language and would spend a lot of time with the students I got to know at the club. The summers in Kiel were the best times, because the town had a good beach. I'd finish work at seven in the morning, get a tram out there, lie in the sun and nod off – or space out, to be more exact – with employees from other clubs. I drank a great deal by then, so after three o'clock, when the students came out, I'd go back to the bars in town to hang out, talking politics, drinking and popping pills until it was time to go to work; the amphetamines counteracted the booze, so I never got too drunk. I often went for days on end without going to bed.

Soon after the incident with John and our money I

moved in with a girl called Victoria whom I'd met in the Star Palast. By then I was going home so infrequently that I'd resigned myself to the fact that my marriage was over, and felt free to embark on another serious relationship. Victoria was a student and from a very wealthy family, so she lived on the smart side of Kiel. We'd always go to very upmarket bars and cafés, which I greatly enjoyed as a contrast from the usual places I'd been frequenting. Victoria's father worried that I'd be a bad influence and tried to buy me off – he actually approached me in the club and asked me how much money I wanted to agree to leave his daughter alone! But after a year in which my most permanent relationship had been with Ziggy's girlfriend – who spoke no English, so it was all sex and sign language – I really wanted something deeper and more stable. I turned her father down and ended up living with Victoria for nearly two years.

As well as being rich, she was very good-looking, sophisticated and loved to hold court wherever she went. She was also a natural flirt, which – as my drug-taking got worse – I started to get paranoid about. One evening I went to meet her at a student club called the Henry the Eighth and found her perched on a stool surrounded by half a dozen guys all drooling over her. When I walked over to give her a kiss she totally ignored me, and as I had enough pills inside me to sink a battleship I saw red. Snapping my fingers I told her to come with me, but all she did was give me a contemptuous look and shake her head. I'd never hit a woman before, but I knocked her off the stool and walked out. When she came to the club later the earlier events seemed to have been forgotten, and we went home together as usual. The next morning, however, I woke up to find myself tied to the bed, and Victoria standing by me with a horse whip in her hand! It wasn't some sort of kinky game, either – she really wanted to hurt me. I moved out immediately and never saw her again.

It was only a matter of days before I moved in with another German girl, Hede. I stayed with her until I left Germany in 1970, when she came to London with me and we stayed together for a further two years. Hede is still one of my very best friends. Strangely enough, ten years later, when I was in New Zealand doing *The Rocky Horror Show*, I got a letter from Victoria. She wrote to say that she was still living alone, and asked if I would like to come and stay with her. It arrived just after I'd been notified of my bankruptcy proceedings and it was as if she'd picked up some vibe that I was very down on my luck. I didn't reply, though, as I wouldn't have wanted her to see me that low.

By 1967 the UK music scene was dominated by psychedelia, but it hadn't reached the northern German ports yet. They saw so many rich American seamen their influence was the strongest, and so the soul boom continued. As we were so well in touch with that music and were one of the few bands with a four-piece brass section, our spectacular handling of Sam and Dave, Otis Redding, Wilson Pickett, Joe Tex or James Brown covers spread our reputation far beyond Kiel. We travelled all over the country doing week-long engagements and the Star Club in Hamburg – the one place we desperately wanted to play at when we lived in that city, but who weren't at that time interested – was now booking us for a month at a time. They paid good money, gave us weekends off because they had big-name acts on then, and put us up in a room each in the annexe of the hotel next door. It was during one of those engagements that Gene Vincent tried to kill me.

After about 3 a.m. the prostitutes on the Reeperbahn stopped work and came into the Star Club for a drink. It was very fashionable for them to have toy boys whom they'd buy presents for, give money to and treat very much as if they owned them – perhaps as some sort of reaction to the way they were treated by their pimps. Young British musicians were considered the best catches, and one of the girls really had her eye on me. She was always sending me bottles of champagne, but I wouldn't have anything to do with her. However Gene Vincent, who played the Star Club regularly, was in love with the same woman and became insanely jealous when she ignored him in order to chase me. Gene was not a man to get on the wrong side of; he hadn't been too stable since being in the car crash that had killed his best friend, Eddie Cochran, in 1960. By now he was drinking very heavily – he's the only man I've ever seen drink a whole bottle of whisky without taking it away from his lips – and he was obsessed with guns.

One Saturday night Gene came off stage and couldn't see the woman he loved in the club. He asked where she was, and when he was told that I'd taken a girl back to my room he assumed it was her. Already blind drunk, he flew into a rage and went to get his pistol. I heard him thump up the stairs on his bad leg, but, unaware of what had gone on downstairs, didn't think anything of it until he started to bang on my door and shout for this woman. When I told him it wasn't her but someone else in there with me he called me a liar and started to shoot at me through the door. As the girl and I rolled off the bed I felt the wind from a bullet whizz past my eye, and I still don't know how we made it on to the floor without being killed. The next thing I heard was the sound of Gene being dragged away, but I was taking no chances and pushed the wardrobe up against the door. The next day he behaved as if nothing had happened. He'd obviously been too drunk to remember, but I kept my distance from him after that.

The Bostons were by now in great demand, so Wotilla went to great lengths to hang on to us. He paid me £500 per week, with each member of the band on a good whack too, and – the arrangement I was most pleased with – I had my own dressing room. It used to be a a store room and still had beer crates stacked in it, but it had a sink, a mirror and a hanging rail and I didn't have to vacate it for anybody – all the big-name acts that came to the Star Palast had to share my dressing room! Bill Haley was the first: he came in and asked me if it was all right to hang his jacket on my rail. I was totally blown away. Later on I asked him why a star like him was still touring at places like the Star Palast, and he told me, 'Son, somewhere in the world there's always somebody who wants some rock 'n' roll. The least I can do is be there to give it to them.' I was so naïve it never occurred to me that he might be skint, but it was such a good answer that in years to come I used it myself instead of admitting I had to work anywhere that would pay me. A year later Jimi Hendrix shared that room with me. He was the most stoned person I've ever met: very polite, almost humble, but so out of it I couldn't understand anything he said any better than I could understand his music.

In 1967 we went to the Middle East for three months. One of the band knew the designer Anne Lambton, who was presenting a fashion show at British Trade Week in the Lebanon, and he'd talked her into hiring the Bostons to provide the music for it. They didn't really need a singer, but I went along as MC. We flew out there with Anne, the designer Michael Fish (whom I knew from *Ready Steady Go* days, when I'd hang out in his shop but could never afford his shirts), Lord Alexander of Tunis and a dozen stunningly beautiful models. We finished the show the day before the Six Day War began, and from our hotel in the mountains outside Beirut we could see Israeli shells destroying the city. The journey to the airport was one of the most terrifying experiences of my life. We were riding through the crossfire, and when we arrived not all of us could get on the flight to Cyprus, where our next show was. A few of the band and I were stuck there for several hours until we could get a flight out, and we were so frightened we honestly believed we were waiting to die.

The show toured to various luxury hotels throughout the Middle East, getting sponsorship from the British Embassy in whichever country we set it up in. Most of my time was spent swanning round in the sun by the pools at the swish hotels and fooling around with the models, but there were a few other worrying moments. When we crossed the Turkish-Armenian border a group of Armenian soldiers forced us at gunpoint out of the coach and made us empty our pockets. They just took everything we had, which in my case wasn't much – but Lord Alexander lost a lot of cash and a very expensive watch.

One night in Jordan, the British ambassador took us out into the desert to have dinner with a Bedouin tribe. It was a very grand feast, consisting of about eighty dishes prepared from every imaginable part of a lamb. As a finale the eyes were brought out in tiny bowls of oil – one was served to the sheik, and the other put in front of me. I was repulsed, but was told it was a great honour to be given the other eye. From the way the sheik had been leering at me through the meal I was convinced I'd been picked because he fancied me. Anyway, after eating everything from sheep's brains to sheep's balls I drew the line at an eye. Not even for Britain! Everybody was looking at me while I looked at the eye. Eventually the Ambassador leaned over and told me if I didn't eat it would be considered such an insult he couldn't be held responsible for my safety. Seeing the old sheik still grinning at me began to scare me, so I picked up the dish and downed it. My stomach rebelled and I had to rush outside the tent to throw up. As I bent over retching, the sheik crept up behind me and grabbed me through the legs! When I started to scream at him to fuck off, he hooted with laughter and went back inside. It was only when I re-entered the tent, feeling very nervous, to find everyone wetting themselves with laughter that I realised the whole thing had been a put-up job between the sheik and the ambassador!

In 1968 we began to work in Britain again. John would fix us up with dates at Irish clubs in London, but the money was always terrible so we'd rush back to Germany where we were living very comfortably. It was on one of these visits that I got back in touch with Mike Leander. By then he had left Decca and was head of A&R/in-house producer at MCA. He was doing well, having just produced John Knowles's big hit 'If I Only Had Time', as well as writing for Tom Jones and Englebert Humperdinck, the two biggest-selling singles artists of 1967. However, he had set himself a rule not to produce anything he'd written. He preferred to sell his songs to artists at different record companies, which meant recording demo tapes in a way that would do them justice. He needed a pool of singers with different vocal characteristics. Elton John – when he was still called Reg Dwight – was used for the lush ballads; David Essex would handle all the bright pop stuff; and I was added to the list as first choice for the raunchy material.

Mike quickly got to like the way I sang, so I'd let him know every time I was in London and he'd contact me to go into the studio with him. What attracted Mike to my work was my rhythm-based approach to singing which, because he had started as a drummer, he found particularly appealing. Also, although he was now a record company executive, he wasn't nearly as stuffy as this might imply. He hadn't lost his rock 'n' roll attitude, and I used to bring it out.

After a few visits we progressed from recording demos to making an actual record. In our first collaboration, which took place in 1968, he showed himself to be very much the record business craftsman; he'd watch the charts closely, then tailor his work to fit the fashions. Our first record was 'Musical Man', Mike's attempt at a Traffic-type sound which was woozily weird with a lot of strings. I don't think either of us was too comfortable with that style, but it was released on MCA. I used the name Paul Monday, for no other reason than that we recorded it on a Monday. It wasn't a bad record but it sank without trace, although we revived it on B sides over the next two years.

I returned to London a couple of months later and we tried something that was much more my style – a funky dance track, 'Soul Thing'. It was an instrumental to which Mike wrote the lyrics, every second word of which was 'boogaloo', the buzz-word in American soul records at the time. We were really pleased with it, and when it came out in August, because it was so close to the style I was already known for, I reverted to the name of Paul Raven. We thought it had a lot of potential as London night clubs started playing it immediately, but sadly MCA didn't know how to market dance music so it didn't sell.

'Soul Thing' was an important record for Mike and me, because while we were making it we began to find a balance between ourselves in the studio. There was a real softness to his approach; he liked a lot of strings and as ethereal a sound as possible, while I was tough and direct, relying on energy more than anything else. It was a good combination – he sweetened me down and I toughened him up. Mike used to joke that I was the rock and he was the roll. I'd try to get him to relax when making records, to take off his Mr Record Company hat and forget the safe option of imitating what was already in the charts. We never forgot the actual song, either, because in 1971 we recycled its melody line to make up the verse of 'Rock 'n' Roll, Part 1'.

I spent a lot of that summer in London, and while I was away the German music scene began to change. During 1968 – a year later than in the UK – the psychedelic invasion spearheaded by Jimi Hendrix and Cream had arrived there, and by the beginning of the next year it had wiped out soul music. Because I had been away so much, it seemed to me as if it had happened overnight; suddenly the sharp-dressed kids all looked like ragbags, with very long hair and beards. It was no longer fashionable to pop pills and dance all night, either – everybody was smoking dope, which never did agree with me, and wanted to sit around and nod their heads to twenty-five-minute guitar solos. Virtuoso musicians were the big draw, so opportunities for singers were limited and I felt very left out. A new circuit of live venues had sprung up, too. By 1969 the bigger places we'd worked at – the Star Palast, the Top Ten Club and the Star Club – were empty, and we were too late to get in on the psychedelic scene because the bands who were in it from the beginning had it sewn up.

We had to travel to find work, therefore, and even that was drying up for me. The band were all very competent musicians and were willing to adapt their approach and get jobs at cabaret venues, but I wanted to avoid that at all costs. Singing cheesy versions of whatever happened to be in the Top 20, while an audience who didn't really care about music ate their dinner, wasn't how I intended to end up after ten years of hard graft – it would have been worse than the variety tours I used to do.

So when I was offered a job as a DJ at a new club in Kiel, the Spectrum, I took it, even though it meant giving up singing. The chap who owned the place, Christian, was a permanent student who'd been at university in the town and had never really left. He had quite a bit of money, though, and until he opened the club he had spent his days hanging round the

campus getting very stoned and engaging in rambling
discussions about the state of the world. He was really
in tune with what the new audience wanted, and as
well as getting the club's music policy exactly right he
also fitted the place out with a huge lighting rig,
strobes and projectors. Our arrangement was that I
DJ'd the early session while he worked behind the
bar; then at ten, when *Umsatz* began, we would swap
over. The very young crowd still liked to dance, so I'd
play soul music; then after curfew, when the students
came in, he could cater for their tastes. I didn't mind
serving behind the bar at all; my approach was one
for the customer, three for me! We'd make regular
trips to London to buy records – terrifying journeys,
because Christian would drive permanently out of his
head, but at least it enabled us to stay ahead of
German release schedules with the freaky groups
while I could seek out obscure soul and reggae. We
became very specialised, so the older crowd who had
once come to hear me sing now came to hear me play
records. Christian's sound 'n' light show was another
major attraction. Between us we built the Spectrum
into one of northern Germany's top night clubs.

Mike and I didn't make another record until
September 1969, and then it was a classic piece of
Leander opportunism. It was just after the Isle of
Wight Festival, where the most popular song had
been the traditional 'Amazing Grace'. At the same
time, next door to MCA's headquarters in Piccadilly
was the first widely publicised squat – a group of
hippies had taken over one of the large houses,
decking it out with banners and playing loud music all
the time. It was constantly in the news, so Mike came
up with the idea of writing new lyrics for 'Amazing

Grace' which would draw attention to the plight of the homeless. Co-written with Eddie Seago, it was called 'We're All Living in One Place'. It came out under the name of Rubber Bucket, although the reason why has been lost somewhere in the mists of time. All I can remember is that it had something to do with condoms and made us fall about at the thought of it – bear in mind we both used to drink a great deal!

'We're All Living in One Place' was actually an awful record and deserved what it got – absolutely no airplay or sales – but it marked another important stage in the development of my relationship with Mike. It was our first session with only the two of us; he played all the instruments and I did all the vocals, with my voice over-dubbed for the choruses. After this Mike really got the bug to create a good record entirely single-handedly and he began to experiment away from his role as an MCA producer. He hired a tiny studio called Mayfair Sound in South Molton Street – a few doors down from where Vic and I had thrown up that Chinese meal seven years previously – and we used to go in there to fool about and see what we came up with. These are the sessions that mark, technically, the birth of the Glittersound. Mike devised a way to make tape loops of his own drum patterns that he could then drum along with to create the big beat. In fact, the two songs we worked on at Mayfair both resurfaced in the seventies. The first was 'Famous Instigator', a rockabilly number that didn't get past demo stage then, but was later used as a track on my first album, *Glitter*. The other, 'Shag Rag That's My Bag' – the first song Mike and I co-wrote, even though I didn't get a credit – contained the rhythm ideas we used for 'Rock 'n' Roll, Parts 1 & 2'.

It had exactly the same hook and, while we knew the theory was right, we didn't put the whole thing together correctly, so although it was intended as an MCA single it never got released.

A few weeks after the Rubber Bucket record came out I dusted off the name Paul Monday and put out a version of George Harrison's 'Here Comes the Sun' which Mike wanted to do simply because he liked the original so much. He played all the instruments and I sang it in falsetto – again his idea, which he claimed was to make sure his version was as different as possible from the original. I tend to think, though, that it was because the BeeGees had made falsettos fashionable. The record didn't turn out very well – my falsetto isn't particularly convincing – and was another non-seller.

Although we weren't being commercially successful, the time we were spending in the studio together meant we were constantly developing as a team. To work with somebody as much as that on something you both care so deeply about eventually brings you closer together than a married couple, and by now we knew each other really well. I'd learnt a great deal from him, as he's an excellent arranger: he taught me a lot about the structuring of songs, and how to make all the difference by putting little touches here and there. On the other hand I helped him by convincing him to take more chances, so by this point he was really enjoying trying to make records that weren't obvious chart fodder. I knew it would only be a matter of time before we came up with the right song at the right moment. Consequently, in Germany during the following year I couldn't really concentrate on what I was doing. I felt nearer than I'd ever been to making it as a singer in Britain, which was still my ultimate ambition.

In late spring we recorded a cover of Sly and the Family Stone's 'Stand', which meant a great deal to me as I believe that group was the most important thing to happen to pop music since rock 'n' roll. With the exception of James Brown, they were the most exciting thing around – Prince, Michael Jackson, Earth Wind and Fire, so many modern soul acts owe a massive debt to Sly. I though 'Stand' was one of their best tracks, so I was delighted when Mike proposed doing it and relieved that the session wasn't going to be anything experimental: he'd booked a full band, plus the three girls who did all Joe Cocker's backing vocals. We approached the song as faithfully as possible and I thought we did very well, although we were never going to capture the excitement of the original. Released as sung by Paul Raven, it was another flop. However, it proved to me beyond any shadow of a doubt what Mike and I would be capable of together if we stuck at it. All through that summer I yearned to be back in England on a permanent basis.

The one obstacle to my moving to London was my girlfriend Hede. I tried to persuade her to come with me, because we'd become very close in Kiel and I didn't want to leave her. In a mercenary way I also knew I'd need somebody to support me while I devoted my time to music; I used to tell her I was thinking about *us*, but I was thinking about *me* nearly as much. For months she refused, saying she didn't want to leave her twin sister who worked in the theatre in Kiel, as she was her only relative in that part of Germany. Eventually, however, I persuaded her to come for a holiday. We stayed in Mike's luxurious new apartment opposite Green Park in Mayfair for two weeks, and as he was composing film music he locked himself in one of the rooms, giving us the run of the place. Hede fell in love with London, as I was sure she would. She had a complete change of heart and couldn't get back to Germany quickly enough to sort out her affairs before moving to the UK with me.

We rented a flat in York Street, just off Marylebone High Street – even though I had no money at all, I still had a lot of front. It was just one large room in a house that's now a hotel, and we – or rather Hede – paid £15 per week for it. She was fluent in several languages and got a job as a translator for a steel company. The only one earning steady money, she virtually kept me while I tried to get my recording career off the ground, most of which consisted of going out on the town with Mike to meet people from the record companies. Mike liked having me around; he was a very shy person and when I first met him he was coming out of a bad marriage, so he was quite introverted. Because I was always outgoing I could chat up the ladies for the two of us. From my point of view it worked out well too, as he always had plenty of money and could pick up the tab in clubs and restaurants.

I also hung out with a group of people I knew through *Ready Steady Go*. They were all connected with the music business and lived in an area of central London bordered by the Edgware Road, Baker Street, Marylebone Road and Oxford Street. If Elvis had the Memphis Mafia, we were the Marylebone Mafia – a cut-price version! Vic Billings, who hadn't managed me for years but still looked after Dusty Springfield and Eden Kane, had an office in George Street and lived in Bryanston Square. His partner Jef Hanlon, who years later became my manager, shared a flat with Karl Green, the bass player from Herman's Hermits, just down the road from me in Upper Montagu Street. Kiki Dee and Michael Aldred, *Ready Steady Go*'s co-presenter until he got sacked, lived in a basement flat in the same street. Dusty lived in Baker Street, and Jimmy Ruffin, whom Jef managed, stayed in a flat in Molyneux Street during his frequent visits to London.

It was a very social scene. Dusty still had parties and people were always in and out of each other's flats, but few of us had any money so every Sunday Vic would feed us all with a huge beef stew. He used to say he felt it was his duty to make sure we had at least one proper meal a week, and in return we nicknamed him Mother Billings. Everybody in the clique would turn up with bottles of cheap Hirondelle wine and afterwards we'd play forfeits, or Monopoly or Risk – board games were a trendy pastime in London then – or sit around just being silly.

The name Gary Glitter came out of one of those Sunday sessions. I've always said that it was invented when I was watching *Rock Around the Clock* with some friends, and wondered what the seventies' equivalent of Bill Haley and the Comets – a classic late fifties' name – would be, but that's not strictly true. And it certainly wasn't the grand event or clever part of a master plan that so many people have liked to think it was. At this time, post-Mod fashions were evolving into what came to be called glam, and the Marylebone crowd, who were a very camp bunch –

particularly Vic and Michael Aldred – with the sense of humour to match, were fascinated by it. It was Michael's idea one fairly drunken afternoon to think up names for the ultimate glam rock act. We started shouting, 'Oooh, I wanna be Stanley Sparkle', or 'I wanna be Terry Tinsel.' Vicky Vomit and – for some reason – Horace Hydrogen were among the other names put forward, but Gary Glitter was declared the winner. Michael thought it up, and it tickled me so much it was given to me as a nickname.

5
Rock 'n' Roll,
Part 1

The period just prior to us making Rock 'n' Roll, Parts 1 & 2' was a strange time for music. There were a lot of MOR records in the charts – artists such as the New Seekers, Perry Como, Tom Jones and Shirley Bassey – Elvis was usually in there somewhere too. The Motown acts, which had dominated the year before, weren't nearly as strong as they had been. British pop seemed to be going through a phase of reinventing itself: a few heavy rock bands left over from the sixties were still having hits, and then there were acts such as Rod Stewart, Slade, the Bay City Rollers and T-Rex just beginning to come through. Music was very much looking for a new style, and hadn't really arrived at anything definite yet.

Very little home-grown music was being played in the clubs. Mike used to pay for us to go to places like Tramp and the Revolution where the music was all James Brown, Otis Redding or Wilson Pickett. We always found what was going on in the clubs a much truer indication of what young record buyers actually wanted. Unlike the radio, which had to cater for the general public, clubgoers were really serious about their music – they went out and paid money to hear it, and if it wasn't exactly right at one place they'd go somewhere else. All through 1971, the most successful discotheques were playing American soul music practically non-stop. I thought it was great: it was the sort of gutsy soul material I'd been doing in Germany and was still doing whenever I got a pub gig – I used to sing in a kind of Joe Tex style. But the sad thing about it was that all the real grab-you-by-the-balls-and-*make*-you-dance music was imported. Kids obviously wanted to dance, but about the only records outside the funky soul soundtracks that were being played in the clubs were the Beatles' 'Hey Jude' and Norman Greenbaum's 'Spirit in the Sky'. There was nothing white happening that was anywhere near as exciting.

What Mike and I were really looking for was to find a white disco sound – something that was made in the UK, and that kids would dance to in clubs; something that could compete with the Americans. But I wasn't looking for something completely new: instead I was trying to adapt the American soul. So Mike thought I was wasting my time. He used to tell me, 'Look, you're not black. So why bother with all that?' But the truth of it was that everything else we'd been trying over the last couple of years hadn't got us anywhere either.

While I was away in Sheffield with the Bostons, Mike had left MCA and joined the GemToby Organisation, GTO. It was an umbrella-type operation founded by Lawrence Meyers, a music business accountant who had seen that a great many producers, writers and artists' managers were in desperate need of hard-nosed advice when it came to striking business deals with record companies. He set up the company in a block of offices and encouraged creative people to become part of it so that his specialised staff could manage their business for them – in return for a percentage – and leave them free to concentrate on the artistic side. Tony McAuley, who had written hits for the Foundations and Edison Lighthouse, had an office; Tony DeFries and his protégé David Bowie were in there; the New Seekers were part of GTO; and Mike worked out of there. It was the nearest thing the UK ever had to a Brill Building or a Motown set-up, with so many creative people working under the same roof on a variety of projects. It was an exciting environment, where people would take an interest in what the others were doing. Artists and producers were always dropping in – Marc Bolan was a regular visitor, stopping by to see David Bowie.

His new situation gave Mike much more freedom to experiment, and he spent every minute of his free time in the studio. He'd frequently take me in with him, and every day I wasn't actually working with him I'd hang around in his office – I was so keen that I didn't want to miss anything. It was in November that we went in to record 'Rock 'n' Roll' and it came about as much by accident as anything else. Even the session happened by default. Mike had studio time booked for David Essex to record demo tapes of the MOR-type songs he'd written, but David cancelled very late in the day. Because the time had already been paid for, Mike quite naturally wanted to make use of it. I was sitting in his office at the time David's call came through, so the two of us went down to the studio. We didn't have a clue what we were going to do –

what we'd attempted before hadn't worked, and at the time we hadn't got any new ideas prepared.

Up until then the only writing I'd done was my contribution to 'Shag Rag That's My Bag', which wasn't that much. I didn't really have the concentration to write by myself, and as nobody had ever made me sit down and do it I'd always assumed I couldn't; I was happy to leave that side of things completely to Mike – until that session. After we had sat around for ages scratching our heads, Mike asked me why I didn't try writing some songs. I was amazed and said, 'You're kidding – I can't write. I don't even know where to start.' But he was insistent that I should give it a try, and just as adamant that I didn't attempt to come up with any sort of funky soul song. The only other sort of music about which I knew enough to use in my first attempt at song-writing was rock 'n' roll, and when I suggested it Mike surprised me for the second time that night by replying, 'Fine – why don't we try some of that?'

I started to turn over ideas for songs in my mind, hoping to come up with a snappy title, then I remembered an article I'd read in *Melody Maker* a few weeks before: the first part of a retrospective feature on rock 'n' roll called *Rock 'n' Roll, Parts 1 & 2*. That was it! Suddenly it all became so completely obvious – write a song called, quite simply, 'Rock 'n' Roll, Parts 1 & 2'. I got really excited and shouted over to Mike that I had the title. He liked it, and from then on it was just like going back to my roots – 'Can you still recall in the juke box hall/when the music played and the world stood still'. While I was writing those lyrics I felt as if I was reflecting on my childhood, and it all came out so naturally. We appropriated elements of 'Soul Thing' and 'Shag Rag' because both had a taste of the natural energy we were looking for, but that apart, nothing that Mike and I had ever done came close to this. It felt like it was what we were *meant* to be doing. By comparison, all the stuff that had gone before – even though we'd tried our hardest – didn't really have our hearts in it. It reminded me of the last gig I had done in Germany, when I opened for Little Richard at the Musikhalle in Berlin. I stood in the wings watching him, and when he came off stage past me I was totally caught up in rock 'n' roll – literally lost in the music. It was still the most exciting music for me and then, like this moment, I couldn't figure out why I had ever bothered with anything else.

Recording 'Rock 'n' Roll' was probably more haphazard than the way we'd written the song, so it was by a series of completely unplanned events that we ended up with what came to be known as the Glittersound. We recorded it on decrepit eight-track tape machines, which kept breaking down and we had to keep ticking them to start them up again. This meant that the finished tape had all sorts of clicks and pops on it. Mike could have edited most of them out, or gone over the worst bits again, but when we played it back we decided to leave it exactly as it was. It gave it that raw energy sound that was missing from British pop music then. The music made it sound like we were working hard. It was a feel that many of the soul records had – they, too, were often recorded really dodgily – and that was what seemed to go down so well in UK clubs.

Our unique guitar sound was achieved simply because Mike couldn't play chords very well. He'd tune all the strings of his guitar to A, with a bottom E to go with it, and play the instrument by putting his finger across the strings on the same fret and moving it up and down the neck. It was almost a slide guitar technique, much like many of the old blues players used. Not having to worry about the fingering meant he could strum across the strings with great power. When this sound was put through his old five-watt valve amplifier – which often needed a kick because of loose wiring – it rattled, resulting in a real dirty growl out of the guitar chords. It sounded like we had a sax playing underneath the guitar chords, and when people found out we weren't using any brass they were baffled. In later years I'd be sharing the occasional line of coke down at Tramp with some of the best guitar players in this country – seriously major guitar players – and they'd ask me, 'How on earth did you get that guitar sound?' Try as hard as they could, they'd never been able to work it out!

Then there was our big beat, a huge drum sound that was very important to what we were trying to do. About eighteen months previously there'd been a record in the charts which had really impressed me – 'Neanderthal Man' by Hot Legs, better known as Kevin Godley, Lol Creme and Eric Stewart, who went on to become 10 CC. It was so brilliantly simple – just great big drums smashing away at the beat and three lines of lyric; pure, raw excitement, and it had got to Number Three. And that was the kind of feel we went for. So Mike used the same looping technique he'd used on 'Shag Rag'; it allowed the snare drum to play on the beat, and he could then play another drum part on another track. Then to boost it up to the point at which it was right up there in front with the guitars, we added handclaps. First we got two pieces of wood about a foot and a half in length, recorded me smashing them together and made another tape loop of that to run in time with the snare – a very crude predecessor of how producers do handclaps with a drum machine at the moment. Then we'd play that back and, on another track, record ourselves clapping along with it, mix the two tracks down on to one and repeat the process over and over again until we'd built up a big enough sound. That was why I always had to use two drummers in live performance – it was the only way I could get close to that sound we created in the studio.

I've always believed that doing those handclaps physically became very important in the way we appealed to people. When you're building up a rhythm track like that, if you use electronics to trigger the sound of a handclap and lay it on top of itself even up to a hundred times it'll sound exactly like the first one did, only louder. But if you've got a track with a handclap on it, and keep adding to it by over-dubbing yourselves clapping along with it, it doesn't matter how precise you think you're being – it'll always be slightly out, and the sound will end up much fatter. It becomes like a gated thing – several sounds connected rather than one exact one. However, because it's just that little bit sloppy, every handclap is unique and it turns out sounding very like the noise of an audience clapping along at a gig. It has a very powerful effect when people hear it on record, because it's such a human sound. Even now I'll still do physical hand-claps for that reason. It can be quite painful, though – after clapping practically non-stop for maybe three or four hours we'd come out of the studio and our palms would be red and raw as though they were on fire. If anybody had tried to shake hands with us we would have run a mile!

Working through GTO, Mike took the tape to Bell Records, where they liked it but said we needed a B side. We were always going to call the other side 'Rock 'n' Roll, Part 2' but didn't know exactly how we were going to approach it, and now we had no money left to do very much. So Mike just remixed the vocal side, but that wasn't enough: we had to make something really different out of it. By then we were really excited with what we'd already done, so we wanted to build atmosphere rather than do something radical that might detract from it. We decided to keep it all as simple as possible and tried to imagine how a live crowd would respond. After that, all the 'Hey! Hey! Hey! Hey!'s just seemed to come as a natural way to keep the feeling going.

And that was the side that became a hit. Funnier still was the fact that Mike and I won an Ivor Novello Award for it as performer/writer! If anybody ever saw the lyrics written down they'd find themselves faced with lines that read: 'Hey! Hey! Hey! Hey! Hey! Ug! Ug! Shhh! Urgh! Uuurgh! Oooh! Hey! Hey! Hey! Hey! and so on. 'Rock 'n' Roll, Part 2' became a very hard act to follow, because most acts which had won an award like that would adopt the same approach as a formula, and our problem was knowing how many 'Hey! Hey! Hey!'s we could get away with. We managed it as the main vocal on three records, but even that was pushing it, so eventually we had to turn our attention to writing lyrics that made a vague bit of sense. Incidentally, somebody's nicked my Ivor Novello statue and I'd love to get it back. I shouldn't imagine I'll ever win another one.

At the time we made 'Rock 'n' Roll, Parts 1 & 2' I was still working as Paul Raven, but because that name was quite well known in the music business we decided against using it. I'd already had so many names I didn't mind another one: I was born Paul Gadd; I'd changed my name to Paul Russell at school; and recorded under the names Paul Raven, Paul Monday and Rubber Bucket. Now I was to become Gary Glitter. There were several reasons for choosing it. It had been my nickname for a while, and if I wanted to wind somebody up I'd always use it to introduce myself. Also, glam rock had triggered off glitter as a fashion statement – that year Ives St Laurent had designed a range of silver glitter brooches shaped like moons and stars, and by then it seemed that everybody was wearing something sparkly on their jackets. It was also a complete departure from all my previous incarnations, and it fitted that record as it was like nothing I'd ever done before. Finally, it was a stage name that was going to determine my attitude: after all, if you're going to call yourself something like Gary Glitter, then you've *got* to be able to do the business every now and again! I'd look in the mirror before I went on stage, see all the glitter I was wearing and know I had to summon up the same glitter, the same flash and showmanship, from within.

Mike and I were so pleased with the song that we played it in his office almost continually, and the reaction from people in GTO was immediate – everybody, from other artists like Bowie and Bolan to the postman and the cleaning lady, would gravitate to our office and ask what it was. I knew straight away it was the best thing that I'd ever done. What surprised me most was that I'd actually done it. Any musician who's been playing for a while can tell when they've done something that clicks completely into place, achieves everything they set out to do and has an extra quality that makes it really attractive. It sends a tingle up your spine, and that's the feeling we got as soon as we listened to 'Rock 'n' Roll, Parts 1 & 2' on the studio playback. We knew it had exactly that special, indefinable something about it – an energy and sound that were unique – and we were sure other people would be able to get off on it.

The record didn't get released until March 1972, however, because the business side had to be sorted out between Mike, GTO and Bell Records, the company that was going to put it out. I did a bit of haggling over my performance royalties, and accepted 3 per cent rather than hold up the record's release. That isn't a good deal on a record that goes on to sell 5 million, but at the time I was never allowed through the door into the finance side of GTO and was completely unaware of how things worked. That naïve arrangement stood until we renegotiated after the first four or five hits. It has left a bit of a bad taste over the years.

When 'Rock 'n' Roll, Parts 1 & 2' was finally released in March it didn't get into the charts until the first week of June. Those three months were among the most frustrating of my life. It broke through in the discotheques fairly quickly – the DJs played the B side, 'Rock 'n' Roll, Part 2', because it was guaranteed to get people dancing. Although the club audience was the one we felt particularly satisfied about being able to impress, we also knew that we needed radio play. Virtually nothing was happening in that area, though. Alan Freeman had played 'Part 1' on his show three weeks running, very early on in its release, but when it didn't move into the charts he gave up with it. Then Stewart Henry, who had a very dance-orientated programme on Saturday mornings – he played a lot of soul and Motown and reggae – used 'Part 2' as the link between records. He timed the record to synchronise with his announcements of what was coming up in the show or would be on next week, and at the end of a sentence he would turn up the volume for the big shout of 'Rock 'n' roll!'

It was this that gave it more of a shove than anything else, and it made the B side, with which so many people were already familiar from hearing it at discotheques, the hit side. That was the side that was being asked for in the shops. And it was bought in sufficient quantities for it to enter the charts at Number Thirty-seven and move up to Number Eight in two weeks. It was only then that the radio producers who pick the records to be played, and who had passed it over months ago, really found out about it and started giving it regular airplay.

I'd been working for years, and now I desperately wanted a hit. My ambitions changed throughout my career: when I was fifteen, all I wanted was my name on a record so I could hold it up to the other kids at school and say, 'Look, that's me. That's my record.' It didn't matter how bad the record was as long as it had my name on it. Later on, I wanted to be able to make my living from music, which I did by playing live. After that I knew I had to start making some *good* records – with 'Rock 'n' Roll' I knew I'd achieved that aim.

When my record finally hit the charts I was more excited than surprised. It really was jumping-round-the-room time! I can remember my initial reaction as, 'Wow! I gotta hit! After twelve years of banging my head up against the wall I've finally gotta hit!' Of course, at that moment I didn't know what it would lead to, but that really didn't matter. It was a hit. I felt as if I'd won the Olympics! I knew what Mark Spitz, that swimmer who'd won seven gold medals, must have felt like. Or why Muhammed Ali wore his Olympic heavyweight medal for days after he got home. Having a record in the Top Ten, and everybody knowing about it, was like my own gold medal.

I was somewhat peeved at first that it was the B side that was attracting attention; it was none too brilliant for me as a singer, because all I did on that side was shout! 'Hey! Hey! Hey!' However, as soon as I came to recognise what a unique sound we'd created with the guitars, drums and handclaps, I thought, 'So what if I'm not really singing?' I didn't even care about the climbdown over the money. And what made the success even sweeter was that it came right after everybody had been telling me I was too old to make it – even Mike Leander, and he was the guy I was working with!

Until 'Rock 'n' Roll, Part 2' entered the charts, Mike and I had only ever thought about it as a record; the live aspect of Gary Glitter simply hadn't been considered. Then the week it stood at Number Eight we got a call to do *Top of the Pops*. Our immediate reaction was panic. We had no band. We knew the actual music would be no problem, because in those days the Musicians' Union's policy on miming was to allow artists two hours to record a backing track. As this was impossible in such a short space of time – the ruling was a hangover from the days when pop music wasn't taken seriously – most acts used to switch the tapes they'd started recording for the show with whatever they'd already finished when recording the single, and that's what we did. But as far as the presentation went, we knew that going on *Top of the Pops* was the biggest break we'd ever had and we wanted to achieve maximum impact. We decided the ideal way would be for me to sing with a large band behind me: few artists appeared on *Top of the Pops* like that – it was either four- or five-piece groups or singers by themselves. But the nearest thing to a band we could organise at such short notice was a collection of Mike's and my acquaintances who knew how to hold instruments! That very first Glitterband was literally bodies filling in the space behind me. Nobody was actually playing – a few of them couldn't play at all, and Mike himself was miming on lead guitar, which is something he doesn't like to talk about these days!

To make the most of what was already going to look different we knew we had to dress the part, so I went down the corridor at GTO to get David Bowie's advice. He always wore very sharp gear, even just to come to the office, so I asked him where he bought his clothes. He told me to go to Alkusura in the Kings Road, *the* hip shop in the early seventies, which sold a mixture of glam clothes – satins, velvets, sequins and glitter – and Eastern-style chiffony stuff left over from the sixties. Everything on sale there was completely over the top: huge flares, jackets with massive lapels and shirts with enormous collars; and it was one of the few places selling shoes with double- and triple-thick platform shoes. David told us it was where all the glam groups got their gear for *Top of the Pops*, so that's where we went to get ourselves kitted out in glitter from head to foot. With my new name, we felt that was our duty; besides, Marc Bolan had at the time been wearing more and more glitter, as had the Sweet, and we simply *had* to wear more than anybody else.

Mike and I wanted a set stage routine too, so that this motley collection would at least look like they'd done that sort of thing before and could carry the act off. But we'd virtually run out of time, so it was on the day of the show that we worked something out in an empty room at the BBC. As there were so many of us – eight counting me – we thought it would look spectacular if everybody appeared to be doing their own thing on their instruments but came together on the 'Hey's and the big guitar choruses. At those precise moments we would jump round as one, so that our backs were to the camera and the audience, and freeze – one of the guys said it was like playing statues at school. When it came to the show we knew it had worked because, although we couldn't see them, we could feel we had got the audience's attention. Turning our backs on the audience seemed quite radical in 1972, but in fact rock 'n' roll artists had been doing it since kingdom come. It broke one of the first rules of showbiz, but then that was exactly what the early rock 'n' rollers made a point of doing. At the time we did it on *Top of the Pops*, it ran against their established guidelines too.

Despite that, there wasn't much reaction to my first

appearance on *Top of the Pops*. Added to which, our record company was too small to have the where-withal to hype the record up before or after the show, so we were more or less ignored. Those papers that did mention it were very cool, dismissing us as a novelty act. In fact, that was much how the public perceived us. The record had had so little airplay it appeared to come out of nowhere: it was a guitar instrumental with mega-drums and chanting, per-formed by eight guys dressed completely in glitter, even in their hair and on their faces. Quite under-standably, no one knew what to make of us. We must have had the right effect on the record buyers, though, because it went up to Number Two the next week. It had an effect on Mike Leander, too, because after that he refused to go on stage again. He was always too shy to be a natural performer, and said we should both concentrate on what we're good at – he'd be the manager and the producer, while I could be the star. I wasn't going to complain!

Now we had a hit, we had to go out on the road with it. That was the way of the music business in 1972 – acts didn't wait for their album to be released before they toured, because getting out there into small venues on the strength of the first hit single was the best way to make sure of a second. That suited me, as I'm a great believer in people rather than television and radio and have always felt that word of mouth is the best possible publicity. To get that you have to let people see you.

During the days immediately after our *Top of the Pops* appearance, Mike's office took enough enquiries from promoters to assure us that the demand was there for me to play live. So we got in touch with Vic Billings and Jef Hanlon and asked them to put some tour dates together, while we set about organising a proper band – one that could really play the songs as opposed to just looking the part. The only group I knew that had the ability and the attitude to play how we wanted was the Bostons; however, not only had I been sacked from them but they'd returned to Germany. I got a number for John from his Mum in Blackpool and rang him. They agreed to come back to do it, provided we sent them their air fare. So the first Glitterband proper was basically the Bostons, with London session players whom Mike knew on bass and guitar and a second drummer called Pete Phipps, who made his living touring with the big-name soul acts when they came to the UK. We had to have two drummers right from the beginning, as it was the only way we could re-create the record's over-dubbed drums on stage.

The first date we did was Melksham Village Hall in Wiltshire, on Thursday, 15 July 1972. We were billed as the Gary Glitter Rock 'n' Roll Spectacular, and our deal was £120 or 70 per cent of the door take, whichever was more – the place was full, so we ended up with £150. We hadn't had time to rehearse the band properly, though, and we only had two songs that everybody knew: 'Rock 'n' Roll, Parts 1 & 2' and 'Money Honey', an old Clyde McPhatter number that Elvis covered. The latter song had practically the same rhythm as 'Rock 'n' Roll', so all we really did was keep a groove going. Our set must have sounded like 'Rock 'n' Roll, Parts 1 & 2' followed by Parts 3, 4, 5, 6 and 7! But the audience went crazy. My presentation was as exaggerated as the band's glitter costumes, and I over-acted all the old Cliff Duffy

Powers/Elvis moves. It was intended as a bit of a send-up, but because the crowd were *Top of the Pops* viewers, fourteen- or fifteen-year-old kids who were too young to have seen anything like that before, every time I wiggled my hips or went into a thrusting routine they screamed.

The day after that we played another one-nighter in the West Country, then travelled to Ely in Cambridgeshire for a show on Saturday night, and finally back across the country to play the Pavilion Theatre on the seafront in Torquay on Sunday. The last date was added as a favour to the local promoter, Lionel Digby, whom I had known since Paul Raven days; it was one of the Sunday rock concerts that he booked into the theatre when the summer show had its night off. In spite of the travelling we had to do to get there, we were very glad to have done so. The reaction we got at the previous dates was very good but they were only dance halls with low capacities; this, on the other hand, was a seated theatre that held fifteen hundred people and so it was going to be quite a test. The place was packed, even the standing room was sold, and the kids went berserk – they screamed, climbed over the seats and ran down the front, far more excited than at the other shows! It consolidated our feeling about what we had started, and from that moment Glittermania became official. Personally I needed this irrefutable confirmation, because in my fifteen-year career I'd never, ever experienced a reaction like it and I had to make sure it wasn't a dream.

It was said by a lot of the music business that our show was just a straight rock 'n' roll parody. I can see how it could have appeared like that – growing up

when and how I did meant that every rock 'n' roll
cliché was deeply ingrained in me. But what we were
doing was actually far more subtle. Our stage act took
something we understood – rock 'n' roll – and sent it
over the top. But we believed completely in what we
were doing *and* we knew that it was funny – you have
to respect something before you can send it up in a
way that is going to turn out at all amusing. We were
definitely taking the piss, but we weren't parodying.
The whole purpose of glam was to reintroduce a sense
of theatre to rock and to have some fun by exaggerat-
ing certain elements of pop music presentation –
Bolan and Bowie were masters of the art. It was a
reaction against the low-key concerts of the previous
years, when groups made out that they were just
being themselves – the 'Hey kids, we're just like you'
approach. That too was an act, but a less obvious act
than glam and so it wasn't questioned. However, as
the seventies progressed a huge section of the British
public showed their appreciation of a bit of flam-
boyancy with their music.

When I got back to London I was elated. My record
had been at Number Two for three weeks – only
Donny Osmond's 'Puppy Love', the third best-selling
single of the year – kept it off the top; and as I was
in charge of collecting the money and paying the
band, I had a huge bag of cash. It wasn't all mine, and
was far less than I'd earned at previous stages in my
life, but having it in my flat was like the cherry on the
icing on the cake! I tipped it all out on the bed, and
Hede and I rolled around on it and threw it at each
other! She was really proud that I'd finally made it,
and I think, after years of supporting me, that she was
very relieved. I was in dreamland, though, thinking

that this was what the next few years would be all about – hit records, sell-out shows and plenty of money! It was all going to be easy, I reckoned, but what actually happened was that I went to work. I worked harder than I ever dreamed was possible, and didn't have a break of any great length until 1976.

During that first weekend of shows, we were approached by Colin Berlin of the huge booking agency MAM – Music Artists' Management – who handled acts like Tom Jones and Englebert Humperdinck. MAM had heard about the reaction to us in Wiltshire, so he'd driven up to Ely in his Rolls-Royce to see for himself and booked us for an autumn tour. We were flattered by the interest, but had to attend to more immediate matters. At weekends, during August and into September, we were playing a series of one-nighters around the country, and duirng the week recording the first album, *Glitter*. When we went back out on the road we had expanded our repertoire to include 'Baby Please Don't Go', 'Donna', 'Sidewalk Sinner', 'Famous Instigator', 'Hello, Hello I'm Back Again', 'I Didn't Know I Loved You (Till I Saw You Rock 'n' Roll)' – most of the first LP – and a few rock 'n' roll classics. But we were still coming up short of the twelve to fifteen numbers needed for an hour-long set and had to repeat things on stage. It didn't matter, though, because we'd moved into the bigger dance halls by now – Meccas and Top Rank Suites – and the crowds went mad for anything that had the Glittersound big beat.

The audiences got wilder during these dates, and we were soon having to be smuggled in and out of places. It became frightening when the second single,

'I Didn't Know I Loved You (Till I Saw You Rock 'n' Roll)', came out in September and coincided with our show at the Mecca Ballroom in Stevenage. The hall must have been way over capacity, because it would have been impossible to squeeze another person in there. It was a hot night anyway and we were wringing wet with sweat before we even got on stage – we all had to take salt tablets. While we waited in the dressing room, we heard how girls were fainting out front and having to be pulled out of the crowd by the St John Ambulance people. Then, when we came on, the crowd lost control and could barely be contained by the club's staff. I could see fourteen- and fifteen-year-old girls getting squashed against the stage, which was the most alarming aspect as somebody might have got seriously injured. There was another kind of tension in the hall too, as Stevenage, like so many of London's dormitory towns, was full of ex-mods and skinheads. They had made up the hard core of Slade's fans, but now they'd latched on to Glitter as well and joined in the chants as if they were at a football ground. It was the first time we'd noticed we were getting a strong male following, and although it was the tough attitude I'd been looking for in the records, when I saw it under these circumstances I realised the potential danger.

By the end of that month, together with Slade we were the biggest draw on the dance hall circuit. Because what happened in Stevenage was being repeated with increasing regularity, we now needed to play the larger-capacity cinema venues that the tour booked by Colin Berlin's MAM agency offered. However, we were far from happy with the way it was organised. MAM had put on their standard tour, which allowed none of the extras we were using in the dance halls: we were expected to use the venues' house lights and sound and not bring any props on stage. The whole point of Glitter was to create something larger than life – a truly Glittering experience – and so I was more than a little upset. Even when we did Melksham we had supplemented the hired lighting rig by adding our own lights on bits of scaffolding pole. Now, flushed with success, Mike and I had all sorts of ideas to turn our shows into spectacles, but to do that we had to have more lights, a bigger PA and larger stages. With Jef and Vic negotiating we had been able to make sure we got what we wanted, but MAM had sacked them and were taking the line that, since nobody else got any of these extra considerations, why should we? At the company's office they'd look down their noses at Mike and me as if to say, 'Who are you two? All you've got is a couple of hit singles and a few shows under your belts, and you want to tell us how to run things.' Because of MAM's lack of care local promoters weren't nagged to make any extra effort, so they simply couldn't be bothered to sort out the health, safety and fire regulation checks necessary to obtain the permits to put on the kind of shows we had in mind.

All we asked was that everybody moved up a gear to make sure the audience got good value for money, but it was a concept MAM didn't seem to understand. Nobody knew how to react to us, so I had to conform to the norm. Since Gary Glitter was meant to be anything but the norm, I felt increasingly frustrated as the tour progressed – it seemed that every time we arrived in a new town there was a new Mr Jobsworth telling us what we couldn't do. I badly missed Vic and Jef and their personal touch, and after we'd seen the tour through Mike and I vowed we would never let ourselves be put in that situation again. We began to set up our own organisation – one that would keep every aspect of Glitter in house and under our control.

6
Rock 'n' Roll,
Part 2

By the end of the year we could look back on a truly amazing six months. In September, 'Rock 'n' Roll, Part 2' reached Number One in America. It had got into the Top 10s all over Europe – in France, the hit was 'Part 1', which particularly pleased me because it was the side I sang on. And it was a hit, though to a lesser degree, in Australia and New Zealand. 'I Didn't Know I Loved You (Till I Saw You Rock 'n' Roll)' reached Number Four in the UK, and then my first album, *Glitter*, got into the Top 10 just before Christmas. The success was consolidated in the Best of the Year listings. 'Rock 'n' Roll' had hung around in the Top 40 for three months and finished up as the eighth best-selling single of the year – above T Rex's 'Telegram Sam'! The combined sales of that record and 'I Didn't Know I Loved You' put me in the Top ten singles artists for that year, up with all the established teen idols like Michael Jackson, Donny Osmond and David Cassidy. This was remarkable, considering I'd only had two records out.

We felt the main reason we'd maintained the first hit's momentum was that we knew immediately what made us popular: we'd established a trademark sound. That's one of the hardest things in the world for a group to do, but when the DJs flipped 'Rock 'n' Roll, Part 1' to play 'Part 2' they did us a huge favour. Side two's popularity left us in no doubt about Glitter's fundamental appeal, because we weren't confused as to whether it was the singer or the singing, or even some other element. Thanks to yet another accident we'd found something that even today is second only to the Rolling Stones and Keith Richard's guitar as rock's most easily identifiable sound: there are very few people over the age of twenty-five who can't immediately recognise a Gary Glitter record.

We nearly didn't get the chance to exploit the sound, though, as we had to fight to get 'I Didn't Know I Loved You' released. We'd written and recorded it at the same time as Mike remixed 'Rock 'n' Roll' because we had the flow going, so we knew it had the same vibe, but Dick Leahy, the head of Bell Records UK, wanted us to follow up with the old Dion classic 'The Wanderer'. He based his reasoning on the hit we'd had in America, and said he thought 'The Wanderer' would be even bigger – he was one of those who saw us as another Sha Na Na. Arguing our case was one of the few occasions Mike and I really stuck together on something. We both believed, unshakeably, that we had found something unique and probably long-lasting because we knew we could write more of it; no matter how huge a hit we might have had in America with 'The Wanderer', we couldn't write another song like that. We won the battle, and went on to show that we were right – we'd struck oil and only needed to dig that bit deeper to keep it gushing.

The good start we'd had in 1972 inspired us to push the development of the Gary Glitter character as far as we could. Mike's decision to step down from performing made a lot of difference, because now we could focus our attention on one figure up front. It meant we thought about the look very early on. I was always a flamboyant dresser, but in my new role I was going to be utterly larger than life. Huge, because I was an Elvis fan and that's how he came over to me with the pink Cadillacs and the lamé drapes. If some kid was going to buy a poster of me and put it on their wall, then I wanted to be a fantasy figure of the calibre they'd never meet on the bus going to school. Gary Glitter had to be seen as a fictional character as far removed from their reality as possible. At that point I remembered what Vince Taylor had told me at the Two I's over ten years previously, and made a rule never to appear in public without wearing all the gear. I was determined not to let people see me as I really was, because their image of me was always going to be much more exciting then the reality.

Even after those careful considerations, though, my presentation went badly off course when Mike tried to force his identity on me. He wanted me to wear very camp gear, like chiffon, which was never going to work because I'm built like a truck driver! With what he had me wearing, and the fashion of the time for guys to wear make-up – considered very outrageous – the press began to call me the Liberace of Rock, which irritated me no end. I did like all the glitter, though – which was just as well, because by 1973 I was stuck with it! – and began looking for ways to toughen up the image. I soon stumbled on something that I adapted to suit myself; if what went into Gary Gliter wasn't exactly an accident, it was only the result of Mike and me collecting ideas from what was happening around us.

One evening I went to see the Jean Genet play *Le Balcon*. It's set in a whorehouse where the customers are just ordinary local men, but to make them feel important when they're there the girls dress them up as army generals, archbishops, chiefs of police and so on. To add to the bizarreness this production had put them on stilts with great big shoes, and designed the costumes with enormous shoulders. The figures on stage were practically triangular, and when viewed upwards from the audience they looked sensational. I had that fixed in my mind when I went to Alkusura, and kept asking for bigger and bigger shoulders and higher and higher platform shoes. As my costumes got increasingly wild, made in glitter or sequins or foil, I began to see the space-age aspect of them, so I started slanting them towards the sci-fi comic look. What I wanted was a bit of beef – all exaggerated muscles, which you need if you're wearing glitter and want to retain any effect of strength. I stuck with that look, because it was precisely the right alternative to the initial, rather airy-fairy appearance I'd had in my first publicity pictures.

The hairy chest was an important part of the look, and that wasn't planned either. I've never liked wearing shirts and ties – because I'm so solid round the neck and chest I find them very constricting. I'd always leave my collar undone, but Mike would tell me to do it up, saying that nobody wanted to see my chest. Then, one day, when I was going to a photo shoot, I wore a silver fishbone on a chain round my neck. A fan had sent it to me and I wanted to show it off, so I insisted on leaving my shirt undone. We got hundreds of letters asking me to show a bit more of my chest, and I took it from there. I never wore a chest wig, though.

The stare comes from my grandmother back in Banbury, who would always shout at me for squinting – 'Open your eyes up, boy!' she'd yell every time I walked into a room. I wasn't actually squinting – it's just the way my eyelids hang; but her nagging made me open my eyes ridiculously wide. I had no idea I was still doing it twenty years later until I saw a playback of that first *Top of the Pops*! I'd never seen myself perform before, and every time the camera moved in on me I seemed to go into this manic-looking stare. It was quite shocking, and I realised that if I did it suddenly, at certain points in a performance, it could be used to great dramatic effect. The next time we went on the show Mike asked the director to position a camera at the side of the stage specifically for close-ups. Playing to that camera was my way of directly involving the audience at home, which not many performers on that show thought about. It must have had quite an effect, too, because the stare is something that everybody knows. Even today, when the paparazzi want a picture of me they'll start shouting, 'Go on, Gary, give us *the look*!'

As soon as we began to establish my personality, everything we did in the recording studio was tailor-made to support it. The records were designed specifically to be performed on stage; nothing was recorded merely to be listened to, and 'Rock 'n' Roll, Parts 1 & 2' is the only record of mine that's been a hit purely on the strength of what it sounded like. We wrote them as part of the act, visualising what I'd do when performing them and building it up from there. 'Leader of the Gang' came about because the band and I would always start with our backs to the audience as if we were all going in the same direction – a gang with me as the leader. Some songs were even based on things I said on stage: every time I came back from a costume change I'd say, 'Hello, I'm back!', so we wrote a song round that and put it out as a single when I arrived back from a tour of Australia. Just as 'Do You Wanna Touch' derived from the times when I'd lean over and shake hands with the kids in the front row. We'd always incorporate bits where I punched the air and shouted, 'Oi!', and every chorus we wrote was meant to be for the audience. It was nothing more than 'Hey!', because I wanted mass participation so that everybody – us and them – could identify with each other. We were the Gang.

Although my songs were really nothing more than nursery rhymes, the chants would sometimes take hours to write. Just something like 'Hello! Hello! It's good to be back' was fantastically complicated to structure. It had to keep time with the beat and be easy enough to sing along with, but not so simple that the audience got bored. Often I'd come up with lyrical hooks that sounded good as titles and then we'd have to write a song to fit. It was a method that once nearly got us into trouble. In the summer of 1973, while 'Leader of the Gang' was still at Number One, Dick Leahy phoned and asked Mike what the next single was going to be. It wasn't due for another couple of months and we hadn't had time even to think about it, but there was a strike at the record label printers and the company were having to send the work abroad, which took much longer. Mike promised to ring back, then shouted over to me asking if I had any ideas. I'd always been fascinated by the title of the Elvis record 'I'm Left, You're Right, She's Gone' and had been playing around with phrases like that for a while, so I shouted back, 'How about "I Love You Love Me Love"?' He phoned it straight through to Dick and we panicked – with a title like that it had to be a ballad, and we'd never had one out as a single! We wrote it, though, and it entered the charts at Number One – something even the Beatles never did – and became my first million-seller in the UK.

Every single came with an image, too. My costume, the band's, our props and a routine combined to create a unique visual package to perform on *Top of the Pops* – there were no videos in those days, so this was the only way I could make sure each song had its own identity. The fans really appreciated it, and I still get people talking to me about a particular record's look that they saw on *Top of the Pops*. We had more than our fair share of problems getting the BBC people to do anything for us, however. Our attitude was that this was the great BBC which could do anything, and all we wanted was to be creative, not to trot out the same thing week after week. From 1972 to 1975 I practically had residency on the show, but some of the arguments we had made us feel as if we were on that MAM tour again: if it was outside their usual brief, the technicians didn't want to know. The most awkward occasion was when we asked them to make a moon for me to lie on for 'I Love You Love'. Even when we offered to pay for it they wouldn't oblige, so we kicked up an almighty fuss. We got snotty and pointed out that since the single was

Number One and the show was called *Top of the Pops*, surely that song was what it was all about. Eventually they relented, and it was worth the struggle because me lying on that glitter moon has since proved to be one of my best-remembered entrances.

It did get a bit too showbiz at times, and although I knew the glamour was very popular I was never comfortable with anything too camp. The costume which I felt gave me my best identity was the 'Leader of the Gang' leather jacket with the chains on the shoulder – a bit of glitter thrown on to something streetsy. It had a lot of rock 'n' roll about it and was the kind of thing the real hard-core Glitter fans liked. That following had stayed with us since our dance hall days, because the shows had a tight, tribal atmosphere about them which we encouraged. Without being in any way political – because it was just sheer good fun – Glitter was a movement. People came to our concerts dressed up, and participated in more ways than just singing along with the songs. It was powerful, like supporting a football team: Spurs or Arsenal? Glitter or Slade? It was a sense of allegiance that has gone a long way to accounting for my longevity, too. People still turn up at the shows today wearing clothes they've kept in a drawer for nearly twenty years, in the same way that a guy who doesn't go to matches any more will check the results every Saturday to see how his team got on.

By taking Glitter out to the dance halls in the beginning we appealed to the lads, the young working-class men who went out on a Saturday night for a few drinks, a bit of a dance and maybe pulled a bird. At the start of the seventies they were vastly under-represented in the pop world. The acts that record companies were falling over themselves to sign were wearing denim, with hair down to their bums, and making concept albums. These bands were taking themselves more and more seriously and refusing to do dance halls or clubs, insisting on putting on concerts to show off their musicianship. The music press, which was by then an increasingly middle-class, university-educated stronghold, supported this attitude. And the BBC was completely stitched up by the old school tie brigade – it still is – and never had any time for anything that was remotely street. While the record companies were happy to make quick money out of the dance hall crowds, nobody wanted to be seen taking them seriously. It was a ridiculous attitude, because working-class lads have always been the biggest record buyers. They spend more money on entertainment than anybody; it's the same in the cinema – the year's highest-grossing movies will be action films starring Arnold Schwarzenegger or Bruce Willis. The lads want heroes and aren't ashamed of it, and they need a bit of escapism after a boring week in a factory. I've always understood that, so Glitter had enough aggression and glamour to give them both.

To keep our operation going the way we wanted, we had to run things ourselves. So we set up Rock Artists Management – RAM. In control were Mike Leander on the creative side, Ray Brown – a very wealthy solicitor who wanted time off to play rock 'n' roll for a few years – who put up the money, and a successful solicitor called Bob Lowrie, who handled the business aspect and became a very good chief executive. Vic and Jef now had a company operating as Billings Hanlon Management, which we bought out and brought in. RAM moved into offices in Regent Street and was equipped to handle everything – management, promotion, booking, production, business and legalities – and Mike struck a deal with Bell Records to put out recordings.

The new company was built entirely on earnings from my success, and my biggest mistake was not making sure I had any say in what went on there – I was much too busy recording, performing or doing press and promotion. I did try, though, and early on Mike and I had a huge row. He maintained there was no way I would have the time to know what was going on, as I couldn't possibly expect details of every phone call that came into the office. He told me to concentrate on what I was doing as that was my skill – without it there would be no company, and with no company I wouldn't be able to do it so well.

That made sense to me at the time, because it allowed me to get on with what I enjoyed most – naturally I had no idea how things were going to turn out, and I will never know if anything would have turned out differently if I had got involved in the business side. At RAM my working relationship with Mike carried on as before, but now we dreamed of building the self-sufficient rock 'n' roll empire that would one day take Glitter to world domination status.

With everything in place – the character, the office, the music, the Gang – the last thing we had to do in order to consolidate Gary Glitter was lay my old personae to rest. Mike maintained that if I was going to be Gary Glitter it had to be a full-time job, not something I put on and took off. Life was beginning to get complicated in that area, though, because so many people in the music industry knew me as Paul, and the press would ask me about what I had done before 1972. But since we wanted to move forward with Glitter, it would only serve to confuse a whole generation by bringing up my past – as far as most of my fans were concerned I hadn't existed before 'Rock 'n' Roll, Parts 1 & 2', so there was no point in suddenly introducing them to Paul Raven and all the others.

Paul Raven had been a bit famous too – I still get asked for his autograph – but now he was getting in the way so we decided to get rid of him once and for all. The first thing we did in 1973 was to bury him, along with Paul Monday and Rubber Bucket and Paul Russell, at sea. Originally it was going to be in Highgate cemetery, but we figured that would have been too macabre – totally out of order. On top of that we were making a ceremony of it and having a huge party for the press with a champagne buffet – we could hardly have booked the back room at the mortuary for a piss-up. In the end we opted for a watery grave and hired HMS *Belfast* for the reception. Alan Freeman was presiding over the affair, with Caroline Rampling as guest of honour, and we put all the old records, photos, press cuttings and any other paraphernalia we could find into a coffin and lowered it into the Thames. But nobody had bothered to find out how these events are carried out and we'd used an ordinary coffin, which didn't sink. It just floated off down the river, and for all I know, if it didn't wash up on a beach in Holland, it's still floating round the world!

I didn't have my name changed by deed poll like

Elton John because I didn't think anybody was going to nick the name Gary Glitter. Both names are on my passport: Paul Gadd, professionally known as Gary Glitter; I've got credit cards as both, too, so if I fancy a bit of extra service I'll book airline tickets in the name of Gary Glitter. Strangely enough, in spite of the fact that the burial of my earlier personae was just a publicity stunt, afterwards I genuinely felt as if I had broken from the past and the future became much more clear-cut. Without wanting to sound pretentious, it was like being born again.

There was no Christmas tour back in 1972 – in those days the touring circuit closed down between November and February because the entertainment industry's year was structured around putting on pantomimes almost everywhere that had a stage. I did a few one-nighters in ballrooms over the new year – back then it wasn't so much a case of putting together a tour, more making yourself available for bookings – but not many because the crowds I was drawing were far too big for that type of venue. As soon as the pantos were over we went out on the first-ever RAM Presents Gary Glitter Tour, which we played solely in theatres and concert halls – no clubs, dance halls or cinemas. That was something we couldn't possibly have done with an outside agency because concert touring wasn't yet established in Britain, and it was assumed that an act needed to be huge to make the step from, for instance, Sheffield Top Rank to Sheffield City Hall. This wasn't simply because of the latter's larger capacity, but the switch removed the whole social element of a night out for the punter: drinking and dancing until 1 a.m., with a band thrown in as a bonus. By then 'Do You Wanna Touch Me (Oh Yeah)' was out, but we'd still only had three hits – none of which had got to Number One – so no promoter would have believed we could possibly draw a big enough crowd to justify a concert hall tour.

We knew we could do it, though, simply because we weren't just following established guidelines and using record sales as a reference, but were experiencing the Glitter phenomenon first hand. We knew my success was all about live performance and that the Gang would follow us anywhere. At the very worst the first couple of gigs might not have sold out, but because we were handling all the arrangements in-house and could do a spectacular show, we were confident that word of mouth would fill the later ones. However, we didn't even have to worry about that. Jef Hanlon, who was practically teaching himself how to be a concert promoter instead of a booking agent as he went along, did a fantastic job. He took the posters round to all the towns in the back of his car, and liaised with venue managers, local council officials and fire departments to make sure everything was cleared for what we wanted – the motorbikes, lights, smoke, PA systems and fireworks. The entire tour was all but sold out, and we rose to the occasion by giving what I believe were the best performances to date.

The rule at RAM was that everything had to live up to the public's perception of what a pop star should be. It all had to be the best – the most extravagant – and we needed a reliable way to make sure the press knew what we were up to. Up until then my press had been handled by Bell Records, and although they could service the papers with pictures and records and fix up interviews, they didn't have the resources to give the shows any push. In early 1973 we took on a press agent, Tony Barrow, who was invaluable in making sure each tour was an event and that the press was well aware of it. Tony, who had been the Beatles' press officer when they were still based in Liverpool, was by then the classiest, most imaginative character on that side of the pop business. His brief was simple: nothing could ever just happen – every record release had to have a story or some sort of drama behind it, about what inspired us or how we had arrived at a particular lyric, and every gig had to be the most special show in that town since the last time we were there. He devised the presentation concepts together with Mike and myself, and would then get input from the appropriate branch of RAM.

It was Tony's idea to name the tours, so everybody knew that each would be different from the previous outing – nobody else was naming their tours at this time. They were given titles like the Remember Me This Way Tour, the Farewell Tour and the Glitter Over England Tour. Another scheme we hatched to whip up press interest even further was to make sure every tour sold out as soon as it was announced. This would allow Tony to put the obligatory full-page advert of tour dates in the music papers two weeks before each tour with Sold Out notices plastered all over them. The way we ensured that everywhere was full was perfectly straightforward: Vic and Jef would only book us into places we knew we could fill. If there was a choice between doing a 2000- or a 3000-seater venue in the same town, and we reckoned we'd sell 2700 tickets, then we'd opt for the smaller venue. Also, it was common in those days for acts to do 'twice nightly' – 6.15 and 8.30 – shows but we'd do that if the ticket applications guaranteed two sell-outs. Although in many cases we could have got a full house and three-quarters – the extra shows were always very profitable because they involved practically no extra outlay – it wouldn't have been sold out. Ticket demand had to exceed supply, because journalists reading those adverts wouldn't worry about the size of the venues or how many shows we were playing: they'd just see the words 'Sold Out' and realise something exciting was going on.

Everything we'd been planning and hyping came together in March at the end of that first RAM tour, when we did our first show in London. It was a full year since 'Rock 'n' Roll, Parts 1 & 2' had been released, and during the subsequent almost non-stop live work we had deliberately stayed out of London, partly to build up anticipation and partly to make sure we arrived in style by playing somewhere very special. We wanted to play the Palladium, and because we weren't sure how to book ourselves in there – they didn't do rock concerts – we thought we'd have to go outside RAM to promote it. We asked Colin Berlin from MAM for advice and he told us we were mad – no agent, he said, would book us into the Palladium. So we hired it. This was rather impulsive of us and afterwards we wondered if we'd gone a bit too far, because with the kind of show we had planned we *had* to sell out to avoid losing a lot of money.

We filled the place, though there were very few surplus ticket applications, and the show was magnificent – even by the standards we'd already set. Emperor Rosko was the DJ and MC. We picked him because I liked him – his show was the best on Radio

One because he understood music and was a bit of a character. He was also the only one of the station's DJs who went out on the road and played to live people, so he knew how to work a crowd. Springfield Revival were support – they were managed by RAM – but their light, countrified pop was totally the wrong choice and they got howled at by the Glitter fans all through their set.

That show was the first time I used a staircase on stage. We did it because in the Palladium we had the space, and as we were pulling out all the stops we thought it would be in keeping with the place to go a bit Busby Berkeley. (I've had steps at every single show I've done since then, even if it was only two or three.) We hired a staircase from a props department in Pinewood, but we couldn't have measured up the Palladium stage properly because in spite of the amount of room we had the unit was too big – it had to be wedged in place, tilting dangerously towards the front of the stage. I was very nervous before I went on, as not only was it my first London show, but it was also in what was then the most important theatre. I had a few too many gin and tonics to try and settle my nerves – so many, in fact, that I couldn't climb the back of the stairs with my platform boots on and had to be winched up on a chain! When I eventually got up there and the spotlights came on to pick me out, the place went crazy. I was wearing a long cloak with a feather boa trimming and had my back to the crowd. The moment I turned round, I had never heard screams like it – I couldn't hear the music at all. I hadn't rehearsed on the steps because they didn't arrive in time, and as I started to walk down I stumbled. I didn't quite fall, but I wobbled badly and sweat was pouring down my face as the feathers got in my mouth. It must have looked bizarre, and as it happened a huge collective gasp came from the crowd: one second the screaming was deafening, then there was what sounded like a 'Whooosh!', as if they'd all sucked their screams back into their heads. It was truly weird, but it sobered me up instantly, and – through another accident – it made me realise what power I had while I was on stage. I felt I could genuinely control things, and during subsequent shows I'd try all sorts of tricks to get that gasp again. Because we were determined to celebrate the Gang we wanted to turn 'Leader of the Gang', which was becoming our anthem, into something really special. We had *six* motorbikes on stage, all revving up – even one is an awesome sound in a theatre – while I made an entrance on the back of a silver Harley Davidson and launched into the song. It blew everybody away! After the show the Palladium management swore they'd never have another rock band on there: they claimed that during that song they'd actually seen the balconies move!

What that triumph at the London Palladium meant for us was that we'd irrefutably proved our point, and the other side of the live music business opened its arms to us. Suddenly, 'respectable' promoters and theatre bookers who wouldn't touch us before *because* we'd only had four hit singles were looking at us and saying, 'Ooh, he's had four hit singles, where can we book him in?' That's the way they work: suddenly they smell money. For me, the show was one of the high points of my career. The only other moments that came close to it were 'Leader of the Gang' getting to Number One after the three previous records had stalled at Number Two, and 'I Love You Love Me Love' going straight in at the top.

Although promoters and agents were now accepting me as a serious proposition, no other branch of the business was – and this continued all through my successful years. The big record companies, whose money controlled much of the industry, ignored me, because few executives could come to terms with the fact that my success had come about on a tiny record label. This was long before punk, so the independent record label subculture hadn't yet become accepted and nobody in the major record companies liked the idea of people doing well without playing by their rules. Between 1972 and 1974, however, the company I was with, Bell, had the biggest share of the UK singles market: Dawn ('Knock Three Times', 'Tie a Yellow Ribbon', 'Candida', 'What Are You Doing Sunday'); the Partridge Family; David Cassidy; the Bay City Rollers; Barry Blue; the Drifters; Showaddywaddy; the Glitterband; and me. In 1973 they had six of the year's Top 20 selling singles – four of which were mine. It made the big labels feel insecure – they could see there was a lot of money to be made and they weren't getting a share of it. The success of artists working for independent companies wouldn't actually get rubbished, but at every opportunity they'd get sneered at as flashes in the pan, in much the same way that Stock Aitken and Waterman were talked about dismissively in the late eighties. I believed twenty years ago, and still do today, that the smaller labels are much more in touch with the market and can respond to trends more quickly than the inflexible giants. And if their artists don't appear to last very long, that's because the little companies know exactly

Paul Gadd...

o Paul Raven

ght is the Starpic
oto taken for the
xembourg tour

Paul Raven

5PS63

The burial at
sea ceremony
in 1973.
Alan 'Fluff'
Freeman swin
the incense bu
(Roger Norton

With fellow
mourners at t
post-interme
party
(Roger Norton

er Gary Glitter

In concert, 1973
(Ian A. Dickson)

With Uncle John,
his wife and daughter

itter goes to Hollywood. like Leander (right) and I re met at LA port by a US rd company rep in 1974 (Tim Isom)

eting ucho Marx

'I Love You Love Me Love' (Gered Mankowitz)

when a trend is over. But I'd got so far without the big record companies' help by now that it didn't really bother me.

The music establishment used to talk about me as a one-off novelty act, even when I'd had ten consecutive hits, and I was seen as an irritant that wouldn't go away. I think they still look at me that way. I thoroughly enjoyed the fact that it wound them up; it made my hits much more worthwhile when there was a two-fingers-to-the-establishment element involved. My belief was that there were no rules, and if I could change anything to suit myself I would. That's why Mike and I started our own company – because we wanted to be number one and didn't trust anybody else's way of getting there. Just like at school, I wasn't in anybody else's gang, and when I got my own and started calling myself the Leader I had to lead!

The so-called serious music papers never liked me very much either. The *NME* ran a review of one of my Rainbow Theatre shows by Nick Kent – Mr Sarky of the music press – who said that Brian Eno had dragged him along to see me. He described how the minute it started the audience got crazy and went crazier as it continued, and said he'd never been to a gig like it. Brian had a thoroughly good time, yet he still couldn't figure out why. Nor could he figure out if what I did was actually music. At least Nick admitted he enjoyed it and had a sense of humour about it. But unfortunately he started a whole school of lofty, opinionated journalism and few of his imitators had the same intelligence. They were simply superior and sneering, and chose to run me down because they couldn't categorise me. I made nonsense of all their theories about what is and isn't good:

people *shouldn't* have liked us, but they did. Instead of just relaxing and having a good time, according to those writers it always had to be the *right* good time. This was about the time the music papers started to decline in circulation – I believe they did it to themselves because they lost the plot and fell completely out of touch with what people actually wanted.

They hailed David Bowie as the icon of the seventies, which is understandable as he was a very important artist, but they did it to such a degree that nobody else got a look in. It seemed as if mere record sales – proof that people liked you – didn't count for anything. Only in one year between 1972 and 1976 did Bowie sell a huge number of records – he finished 1973 with 'Aladdin Sane', 'Hunky Dory', 'Pin Ups' and 'Ziggy Stardust' all in the Top 20 albums. Slade had the same phenomenal following that we did – between 1971 and 1976 they had fifteen consecutive Top 20 singles (twelve in a row went Top 5) and five Top 10 albums – and yet, like us, it was as if they didn't count. Since the success of 'Gasoline Alley' and 'Maggie May', Rod Stewart has drawn a large working-class crowd, yet because he'd been in the Faces, Steampacket and the Jeff Beck Group he also had a slightly older, more music-based – as opposed to pop-based – following and could be taken seriously. That was the degree of snobbishness that had begun in the music press in the late sixties, was widespread in the seventies and still exists today. My reaction was just to avoid putting myself in situations where they could criticise me. I knew I could sell records without their coverage, so instead of doing an interview with the *NME* I'd choose to be on the cover of *Woman's Own* – their readers liked me, and it had a bigger circulation.

I did get on very well with daily papers during the first years of my success. In the early seventies they discovered that pop stars would sell papers for them, so they were happy to co-operate with our press officers on our terms and we were quick to take advantage of the publicity. Just like today, both the press and the celebrities were well aware they were using each other, but this was before Fleet Street, as it was then, descended to blatant muck-raking, and during those years it was stars who had the upper hand. Tony would feed them innocuous, ready-made stories about how we wrote particular songs, what I did in my spare time – which was a joke because I didn't have any! – or what sort of toothpaste I used, and I'd back it up with quotes. Sometimes we'd stage situations for them to cover – the coffin in the Thames, for example. I was always very good at giving interviews, so Mike and Tony rarely had to invent a quote. The only occasion on which they would do so was when I was genuinely unavailable – I did get a bit miffed when I read what they had put out, but only because I knew I would have phrased it a lot better! In fact, since Mike knew I could expand on a theme so much better than they could, he'd get quite irritated if I wasn't around. We did make a stipulation concerning photographs, though, and had agreements with papers and magazines that they wouldn't use any that hadn't been approved by Mike – he used to sort through thousands. This was because my weight went up and down wildly and I was neurotic about looking too fat in pictures. Quite often there'd be paparazzi waiting outside a restaurant or a night club when I didn't want to be photographed, but if we told them, 'Not tonight, eh, lads?' they'd always put their cameras down. We knew all of them by name, and they weren't nearly as predatory as they have since become. Also, they knew that we'd never do anything again for whatever paper printed any of these off-the-cuff pictures.

We worked hard to make sure the editors felt they were getting as much of me as they needed, so they didn't need to dig about for anything else. The only time – prior to 1976 – that I came close to falling out with the press was over the question of my sexuality. Journalists were continually asking me if I liked girls or boys, but all I'd ever tell them was that 'I liked sex'. This used to wind them up terribly, so they'd always assume that I was gay. As artists like Marc Bolan, Elton John and David Bowie were busily confessing bisexuality, with all my glitter and make-up I obviously came across as camper than a row of tents. The press believed that by avoiding the issue I was really trying to cover it up, and quite a few papers felt it was their duty to expose me. Mike would get frantic and wanted me to go on record to put things straight, but I knew that keeping silent would work to my advantage. It wasn't just pop stars that were coming out of the closet. In the early seventies there was a new and large gay audience to be considered, and while I didn't want openly to support Gay Lib, because I wasn't gay, I thought that stating a preference for women would automatically deter a big section of my potential audience. After all, Glitter was supposed to be about removing stigmas and breaking a few rules. So I deliberately left that bit of mystery about me, knowing it would mean that both boys and girls could buy my poster, put it up on their bedroom wall and dream about going to bed with me. It was a piece of opportunism, but it came out of not wanting to upset anybody and wouldn't even have been an issue three years previously. I was confident enough about my own sexuality not to worry about what Fleet Street was writing.

I was caught out, however, when the newspapers stopped reporting rumours and started reporting so-called facts. When I arrived in Australia for my first tour the Australian Gay Rights Movement picketed my shows. All dressed like lumberjacks, with big bushy moustaches, they claimed that kitted out in sequins I was setting the gay cause back ten years. A lot of young boys, too, would sneak backstage or con their way into my hotel suites, often dressed as girls and looking very pretty. In the end I had to stop *anybody* coming to see me unless I'd brought them there. There's still confusion today – I meet guys who tell me they've been warned, in 1991, not to drop their car keys in front of me! That was the nearest I ever had to a problem with the popular press, but it still worked to my advantage because as a result I gained a large gay following who have always been among my most loyal fans as they claim I gave them hope as teenagers. When I made my comeback in the early eighties, it was their support which saw me through some really lean times.

There was a healthy rivalry between us and our various pop chart competitors – quite a few good-natured shouting matches went on in the bar after *Top of the Pops* – but on the management level it was a very gentlemanly affair. Mike was always on the phone to Slade's manager Chas Chandler, and to Chin and Chapman who were responsible for Mud, the Sweet and Smokie, to discuss a singles release schedule. Everybody wanted a fair crack at getting to Number One, so there was no point in going up against each other. I personally got on well with the big stars, too. Bowie I knew from the GTO days: I was always meeting him in the lift there, when all he'd ever say was 'Hi Paul!' – he still calls me Paul to this day; Elton John and David Essex I'd known for years, too. I became very good friends with Rod Stewart, and at *Top of the Pops* in 1978 I met Paul McCartney who told me the *Glitter* album was the only tape he played in his car. Guys like the Rolling Stones, the Who and Paul McCartney never saw me as a rival so they could afford to be friendly – there was never paranoia about me like there was between Rod and Mick Jagger, who were continually trying to find out what the other was up to.

Surprisingly, though we were market leaders there were few attempts made to rip off the Glitter sound. If anyone had, Mike would have known about it, because his A&R training made him very conscious of what other people were doing in the studio. However, Slade had established their own sound before us so they weren't going to change, and apart from them it was only Chin and Chapman material that posed any sort of threat. They made the only two records that, in my opinion, ever came close to Glitter records – 'Devil Gate Drive' by Suzi Quatro and Mud's 'Tiger Feet'. But as the artists themselves didn't have any input, they were really only vehicles for the writing/production team. My creative team, on the other hand, was 50 per cent myself; as it was me performing the records I had a say in the whole process and could always put that little bit more into it. That's what gave us the edge to stay ahead of the field.

7

International Incidents

Right from the beginning we had to consider Glitter's international possibilities. 'Rock 'n' Roll was a hit in most European countries and in the United States, but the international market was very different from what it used to be. During the fifties American records would filter through overseas, but it wasn't until the next decade that communications advanced sufficiently in the UK for much music to be exported. At first it was on a European-only basis, and the worldwide potential of groups other than the very biggest couldn't really be exploited until the late sixties and early seventies. Although a record could be released all over the world simultaneously, in these pre-video and pre-HTV days promoting the personality behind the song involved travelling, which was a much more laborious process then. Often acts were forced to pick a region and concentrate on it at the expense of finding sales elsewhere. We all had our own territories; David Bowie, for instance, broke in America very quickly at the expense of Europe; then, when he worked hard to promote himself on this side of the Atlantic, he lost his American audience for quite a while. It happened to the Bay City Rollers, too, later in the seventies – they went to America, then Japan and then back to America, and by the time they returned to the UK their crowds had moved on.

In spite of our first release going to Number One in America and the follow-up getting into the Top 40, we couldn't tour there to capitalise on our success. For one thing we weren't ready: our hit happened before Gary Glitter had ever set foot on a stage, and our act was still developing right up to the third single. For another we were under tremendous pressure from the record company in the UK: they wanted four more singles – complete with B sides – and an album during that first year, and because Mike and I wrote all our own stuff in the studio we needed to spend a lot more time in there than most of our contemporaries. We also wanted to make sure we consolidated a domestic fan base, as we knew that would be the basis on which anything else would be built. Had we disappeared for the six weeks or so it would have taken to make an impression on America we would have come home to nothing. So our territory became initially Europe, and was later expanded to take in Australia.

I sold as many records in Scandinavia, Germany and the Benelux countries as I did in the UK, and 'Rock 'n' Roll, Part 1' was on the French chart for nine months, so my following in Europe was huge. But I did very few tours there because none of those countries had the sort of rock touring circuit we had in Britain and there were few suitable venues – the sports arenas and stadiums weren't yet open to rock shows, the larger venues were licensed clubs which my teenage audiences were too young to get into, and the cinemas and most of the theatres were too small to contain my following. The live shows we did were in whatever cities had large theatres or concert halls – Copenhagen, Hamburg, Berlin, Paris and Stockholm. These shows would always be called Glitter Over whatever city we were in, which was ironic because the original title, Glitter Over England, was conceived specifically to give our home crowd something unique to identify with!

The vast majority of the work we did in Europe was television, as every country had its equivalent of *Top of the Pops*; as with the UK version, we were practically residents on all of them. Because I was on such a perpetually tight schedule we'd fly into a city at lunchtime, go straight to the TV studio, run through the song in rehearsals, perform for the cameras and studio audience in the evening, then go straight back to the airport and get a night flight out. This method worked very well everywhere except Amsterdam, where the director had devised a way of making the group look almost 3D by superimposing different films on top of each other. However, it involved filming from about half a dozen different angles, and as each one took ages we frequently missed the last flight back to England. As I always had to get back for the next morning, we'd have to hang around the practically deserted airport and hitch a ride home in the early hours on a plane that was flying to London to start its scheduled route there. Handy as this was, because there were no other passengers, they'd never turn the heating or lights on – I can't remember how often we'd come through Heathrow at about six in the morning looking like death and wrapped in blankets to stop ourselves shivering!

We were huge in Spain too – so big that in 1973 I won an award for being the most important contributor to New Music, as they called pop. It was quite an honour, as the previous recipient had been John Lennon. What was even more remarkable about our selling records there was that this was during the Franco regime when nobody had a record player – kids would give me singles to sign that were a year old and in absolutely pristine condition because they'd never been played! We never toured in Spain, however, because they had no facilities at all for rock concerts, and we had a bad time when we went there to do a TV show after getting the award. The first thing the producer told me was not to go in front of the camera either with my chest uncovered or wearing make-up. I refused to comply and was ready to go home, but the people from the record company pleaded with me as this was Spain's biggest show. As no one had a record player I couldn't see how this would increase sales, but I pretended to agree. I did the rehearsals and planned to put on my normal costume and make-up in the dressing room but not come out until the last minute. The orders to make me wear a vest and wash my face must have come from high up, however, and nobody was leaving anything to chance – as I stepped out to go on stage my way was blocked by police armed with rifles, who told me that if I went out there like that I'd go straight to prison afterwards! I didn't do the show. It was a matter of principle, and they'd already sent me my award.

The only other time we went to Spain was a year later when we played at Cap 3000, a big televised pop festival in Benidorm which we headlined with the

Faces. We got to play this time, but we didn't look like we usually did on stage and it was entirely our fault. The festival was a three-day event, and during the afternoons the Glitterband, the Faces and I hired a local go-kart track and spent several hours racing each other; however, we weren't very good and kept falling off, so the groups went on stage in the evenings covered in bandages and plasters and with arms in slings!

European television companies used to organise a lot of these festivals during the summer months. We did them in several different countries, and the formula was always the same: they'd book about ten big international artists, the same number of lesser UK groups and about a dozen local acts to open; they'd hold it over two or three days in a big outdoor venue and each act would come on, mime three songs and get off quick. One of the very few times we played in Italy was at one of these affairs – the San Remo Festival in 1975. I didn't sell records at all in Italy, but I got played in the clubs and the year before I'd been voted its Number One Disco Artist. Paul McCartney was supposed to headline, but he hadn't turned up because they wouldn't grant him customs clearance at the airport, so I was promoted to top of the bill. This meant very superior hospitality, and I got so pissed that Demis Roussos had to carry me back to the hotel, all the way up a hill over his shoulder! I was so badly gone I had no idea this had happened until he phoned my room the next day to ask if I was all right – I said 'Yes thanks, except I've got a bit of a hangover.' I was just starting to wonder why he was so concerned when he told me how I got back from the concert!

* * *

Europe was good to us. We tried to make sure they got as much Glitter as they wanted, and weren't really considering opening up another market until the office got a phone call, in late 1972, asking if we'd be free to go to Australia. We'd always assumed it would be about as time-consuming a touring proposition as America, simply because it was so big and so far away. But when we found out that the population was concentrated into so few major cities, and that as the promoter only wanted us to do three of them we could be there and back in less than a week, we decided it was too good an opportunity to miss.

The promoter who contacted us was David Ginges, who is still one of my very best pals. He was then putting on gigs at university student unions and had just got to the point where he wanted to step up to a bigger league. He kept in touch with what was happening in the UK and Europe, was well informed about glam, and although he couldn't afford any of the established acts like Marc Bolan or the Sweet he knew he needed to get in on it. At this stage my record sales were only reasonable in Australia and I was still establishing things at home, but he was convinced we were about to become huge and figured that if he got in quick enough he'd be able to afford us.

It worked very well from our point of view, because when we arrived there in March 1973 we were the first of that wave of seventies' artists like Slade, Bowie, Elton and Bolan – the Australians hadn't had any tours by overseas rock stars since the Beatles in the sixties. So when David was arranging press coverage of the tour – which he took very seriously because he wanted to make his own name too – the media were incredibly keen. Because there were then five TV networks in Australia, and they were very competitive, I was introduced to reporting techniques that were worlds apart from the rather reserved way of doing things at home. Down under, camera crews literally followed me everywhere: they drove next to my car, trying to film through the window; if I went to a restaurant they would bribe their way on to the next table; and when I shut my hotel room door behind me they would be a bit peeved that I hadn't invited them in.

In spite of this coverage, the six dates we played were not a financial success. The Australians weren't quite sure what to make of Glitter – I think most of them took one look and decided I must be some sort of Pommie poofter! To make matters worse, David had booked us into huge ten thousand-capacity venues – I'd never seen halls that big – but advance ticket sales were only about fifteen hundred. At the first show, at Melbourne Festival Hall, it was almost impossible to get any atmosphere going in a space that was three-quarters empty, yet – for reasons they kept to themselves – the Melbourne Police Department had decided to station a line of officers around the stage, facing the crowd. We weren't enjoying ourselves at all, as this was so unnecessarily threatening that it made the audience very subdued. During 'Famous Instigator' I always do a trick where I kick the microphone stand across the stage and run round to catch it – it never fails, and always comes back to me. Except that night. It stuck on something on the floor, toppled over and hit a policeman on the back of his head. I stopped the music dead – the Glitter-band were excellent at responding to my cues – and leaped over to him, apologising and offering him my hand to shake. He wouldn't do it, but just stared at me, and suddenly I realised I was on to a good thing: Australian teenagers were pretty anti-establishment in those days, and the longer the policeman ignored me the more this crowd that had been fairly indifferent up until then came out on my side. I milked it for a while, looking up at the audience and pretending to be baffled, then said to him 'No offence' as cheerily as possible and got on with the show.

When we got to 'Do You Wanna Touch' – the single release that coincided with the dates – I asked if anybody wanted to touch. I appealed to them: 'Who wants to shake my hand? Come on, I've never been to Australia before and I want to meet some Australians.' Nobody moved except this kid in a wheelchair who came down the aisle. He was completely and utterly harmless, but the police would not let him through to shake my hand! The place erupted. The next day the media all reported the incident, raving about the show and saying that I really knew how to work a crowd, and the radio started playing 'Do You Wanna Touch' practically non-stop. Mike, Tony and I could never in a thousand years have dreamed up a publicity stunt that effective, and the whole thing had happened for real. We got a bit more mileage out of it when I had to make a public apology to the Chief of Police because he'd made a statement to say that I'd publicly humiliated one of his officers.

Because of that incident the other shows, in Sydney and Adelaide, were better attended than they might otherwise have been, but nowhere was even half full. So, naturally, we weren't over-anxious to book another tour there – but David persuaded us to try again. He was convinced that we'd won a lot of points there, and if we stuck at it we could be huge.

He was right, but I had no idea how huge until we went back there again towards the end of the year. In Britain during 1973 the level of enthusiasm had moved up a few notches, but nothing could have prepared us for the reception we got when we went back down under. When our plane landed we were told to stay aboard after the other passengers had got off. We realised why when we looked out of the windows to see at least ten thousand kids screaming, wearing glitter and waving banners. I had never seen anything like it before. I had to be taken off the plane on a stretcher and put into an ambulance, as it was the only way they could get me out of the airport. When I'd been transferred to a limousine for the drive into town I found the whole route lined with scream-ing kids. It was the same at the hotel: the police had to put up barriers at either end of the street to keep out the fans. This was also the tour that the Australian gay movement was picketing, and they would stand outside the shows with placards and get set upon by Glitter fans! Before I'd left in March I must have lit the touch paper on a firework, and now, nine months later, it was going off with a bang.

We stayed for nearly a month, played all the same places we'd played before, plus Perth, Brisbane and Canberra, and sold out several nights everywhere. We had five full houses at the Melbourne Festival – which set a new attendance record that has only been broken once since, when Barry White sold it out six times in 1975 – and this time they needed the front-of-stage security because the crowds went wild. It was unheard-of business. I was much bigger than in the

UK because I had no competition down there – other bands still weren't touring Australia, so there was nobody to steal my thunder. The tour was the making of David Ginges, too. He became the most respected promoter in Australia after that, and went on to tour all the big rock acts until he sold the company for a small fortune at the end of the seventies. That pleased me greatly, because David is a lovely man and it was only his faith that got us into that situation in the first place.

My reception there wasn't a passing fad either; once the Australians had taken to me they stayed with me, and I received a gold disc from that country for each album I put out. In return, I toured there at least twice a year and would go there on any excuse. In 1974 I went twice in one week – four thirty-hour flights in six days. I can't remember the journeys at all, as a combination of super-jetlag, general exhaustion and a few drinks meant I was completely out of it! Just before the start of the tour, I was asked to appear on the big Australian TV show *King of Pop* in Melbourne several days before I was due to arrive in the country. At first I didn't think it would be possible, but when they told me David Cassidy was going to be on it too I knew I couldn't let the side down.

After the show I went to my hotel where David Cassidy was staying in a suite near mine. That evening I rang him up and suggested he came with me to the Station Hotel, a famous live music venue, to see a band that had been recommended to me. I told him we could disguise ourselves a bit and sneak past the fans outside to go and have a bite to eat and a bit of fun. But he said no. As I thought he was just being snotty, I decided to wind him up. I looked out of the spyhole in my door and could see that he, just like me, had a security guard on his door. So I phoned down for an extra one and then watched through the spyhole again. About ten minutes after my second man arrived, two more joined the one on his door. I could hardly hold back my laughter as I phoned for two more to bring my total up to four. Very soon three more arrived at his end, and I ordered another five! By now there were fifteen big guys in the corridor – they could hardly move out there. I'm not sure if he phoned for any more, because I went out to see the band!

At the end of the tour we headlined a free concert in Sydney's main park, Moore Park. It was in a natural amphitheatre in front of a crowd of about 150,000 – the biggest audience I'd ever seen. Two songs into my set, the crowd rushed the stage, and because it was a temporary structure and not anchored to anything it overturned. As the crowd surged towards it everybody on stage ran for the back of it and managed to jump off just as it started to tip up. I just threw myself into the first car I saw and screamed at the driver to get me out of the place, but it was too late and we were mobbed. It was absolutely terrifying. The driver couldn't move because of all the kids' feet under the wheels. The roof was buckling as they climbed all over it, and all I could see through the windows were hands, faces and chests squashed up against them. They started to shake the car and I was thrown about on the back seat, feeling like a ten-pence piece that some kid was trying to shake out of a money box. Eventually the police got control and cleared the area.

I've never been so scared in my life, because when a crowd gets out of control like that there is absolutely nothing you can do. I was far more scared for them during that incident than I had ever been before. Ever since a fourteen-year-old girl had died after getting crushed at a David Cassidy concert in London, it was every pop star's real fear. Everybody thought how easily it could happen at one of their shows and we felt responsible – that's probably why David Cassidy wouldn't go out when I asked him. That level of mania – and it was beginning to be the same at home during 1974 – also made me fear for my own safety. I had a guy called Bob Lowrie looking after me, an ex-Olympic rower who could take care of himself, but when we were rushed by a group of girls who were out of control there was nothing either of us could do. We couldn't slug anybody. I've had my clothes completely torn off me and been grabbed very hard in the softest of places, and it hurts.

How nobody got killed in that riot in Moore Park is still a mystery to me. It shook me up badly and I stopped putting myself in situations where it was likely to happen. That's when I really started drinking, because I spent so long in hotel rooms. I'd get very bored, and all there is to do is call up room service . . . again.

I used to stop off for little holidays on the way back from Australia. After the first trip it almost became a ritual; that visit had been so brief that we had some days to spare, and since I'd worked so hard and hadn't slept at all while I was out there I felt I deserved a rest. Also, I thought it was a crime to come all the way to Australia and not see something of the world in between, so we broke our return journey in Bali.

I'd been told in Australia that it was the ideal place for a holiday and that Mick Jagger had just been out there, so Ray Brown, Bob Lowrie and myself checked into the same hotel he'd stayed in. It was an amazing place: a village of separate bungalows built in very traditional style, but with all mod cons like air conditioning, and set in grounds that had streams, waterfalls, bridges and funny little gazebos everywhere – it was like living in a willow pattern plate.

I fell asleep immediately and lost two days. When I got up to look around I was totally unprepared for my surroundings – all I had was Glitter gear; after an hour of braving it out in platform shoes I bought a pair of sandals, but I still had to wander about with great big rolled-up flares which kept falling down to flap in the dust! Balinese women also took me by surprise – they were so beautiful that I fell in love with all of them, especially the girl who worked in the hotel restaurant. After three days of seeing her but not being able to communicate I felt as if I was walking round with a pistol in my pocket! I was desperate to have a woman and so I went to the hotel manager and asked if there was anywhere I could go, or if he could fix something up. I bugged him for a couple of days and eventually one evening he said it was all arranged and a taxi was coming for me. I asked where it would take me, but all he said was not to worry – it would take me there and bring me back. I was so pent up that I took his word for it and went, without telling Bob or Ray anything.

Everything seemed OK as we headed towards the town, but then the driver veered off towards the beach and I began to get worried. After about a mile we turned inland towards the jungle and I started to worry – the night was pitch-black, I was already sweating because of the humidity, it was completely quiet except for the occasional barking dog or chirping cricket, and I couldn't talk to the driver because he didn't understand English; all sorts of things were going through my mind. I mentally calculated the money I had and realised I didn't have enough to buy myself out of danger, so if he was going to roll me he'd probably end up killing me.

Anyway, I didn't want to let on that I was afraid, so every time he looked round at me and grinned I shaped up like Mr Macho Cool, as if I did this sort of thing every day! Eventually I saw a light up ahead in the jungle; as we got nearer it moved away, and we began following it deeper into the jungle. The air around me seemed to have got so hot and clammy by now that I felt I could have grabbed hold of it. This is it, I thought. I'm going to be stabbed. And nobody'll know where to look for my body. After what was probably about five minutes but seemed like an hour we reached a clearing and pulled up. We'd been guided into the clearing by a man carrying a dim lamp, and now by the light of it I could see five guys lined up staring at the car. I was petrified. In the dead quiet I could hear my heart beating and I was literally dripping with sweat – not all of it from the heat. Acting tough, I got out of the car like Clint Eastwood as one of the guys walked towards me. He handed me a warm Seven-up and gestured that I should sit on a big wicker chair which I could barely see because it was so dark. There wasn't a woman in sight – which was just as well because by now the last thing I felt like was sex, and I wouldn't have liked offending someone after we'd made an arrangement. Not in the middle of the night in the middle of a jungle.

I was sitting there just waiting for the knife in the back, when suddenly I heard some giggling from behind me and six Balinese girls were led into the clearing. I was invited to take my pick. But as the lantern was so feeble I could only see one at a time, and by the time I'd got to the end of the line I'd forgotten what the first one looked like, and so I had to start again! In the end I just closed my eyes – not that that made any difference – and chose. She took the lamp and led me off to a corrugated tin shack that I hadn't noticed up until then. I took a look round: in one corner was a pit with two raised feet marks in the middle, against one wall was an iron bed frame with a bare mattress, and sitting on a ledge was a huge lizard. Every Balinese house has one – they're enticed in because they're considered good luck and they keep the mosquitoes down. The girl was very pretty, but when she started to strip off she was wearing the most unerotic fifties-type underwear I've ever seen: the knickers came down to mid-thigh, the bra stopped just below her throat and there was a gap of about half an inch between them! What am I doing here? I thought. I'm in the middle of a jungle with five guys who I'm sure are waiting to kill me, and a girl wearing armour – was there an erection in sight? Then she handed me what looked like a section of a Dunlop inner tube, and I wondered just how much worse this could get. I got on the bed with her and just wanted to get it over with – the rubber was so thick it was standing up by itself. Even before I'd settled down she started shouting the only word of English she knew, 'Feeneeshed? Feeeneeshed?' I said, 'I haven't bloody started yet!' and then the lizard ran straight across my backside! That did it. I jumped up, struggled into my gear and leaped into the taxi, screaming, 'Go! Go! Go!'

The next day at the hotel I didn't tell Ray and Bob about what had transpired, but I obviously still hadn't calmed down because they both asked why I was looking so pale when I'd been sunbathing for nearly a week. This was in 1973, and being able to go off on my own like that, to have adventures, was what I missed most when the number of places I could go to without being recognised diminished rapidly during the coming years.

The period between mid-1973 and mid-1975, the absolute height of Glittermania, would have been the ideal time for us to go to America: Australia had proved that I could win over an audience that was completely indifferent to the glam scene, and that I could stay away for weeks at a time without it affecting my popularity at home. However, after 'I Didn't Know I Loved You' Bell Records in the USA didn't release any more of my singles. It was an American company owned by a man named Larry Utall – Dick Leahy was merely head of the London branch – who was at that time renegotiating his distribution arrangements with the huge Columbia Records in New York. I was a valuable company asset as I was then the hottest-selling singles act in Europe; my only two US releases proved I could sell records there with hardly any promotional support; and the US group Brownsville Station covered 'Leader of the Gang' in late 1973 and had a hit with it, which meant there was a definite interest in my music. Consequently, Utall used me as a bargaining chip by holding back my releases so he could bring me to the negotiating table as a potential earner rather than face the question of 'how much longer I was going to last'.

This may be excellent boardroom politics, but it didn't do Mike and me any good because the negotations went on for so long – from 1973, right through 1974 and into 1975 before any deal was finalised. We were hot everywhere else, and wanted a chance to make it in America before the market there forgot about us and blew cold. I was also personally very keen, because 'Rock 'n' Roll, Part 2' had broken through the black radio stations – in Chicago first, then Los Angeles – before it crossed over to the pop charts. Back then we were asked to go and play a couple of clubs in Chicago, but when the office found out they were black clubs everybody lost their nerve except me. I was very eager because I knew the history of Buddy Holly at the Apollo in Harlem, so I knew it was possible for a white rock 'n' roller to win over a tough black audience, and was disappointed when we didn't go. It was that initial reaction in America that excited me as much as the money we could earn there, because the black crowds were the people whose music had to have spirit to it, and they were the ones who went out on a Saturday night to enjoy themselves – exactly the appeal I wanted Glitter to have.

Through the second half of 1973 and the beginning of the next year we knew Bell USA wasn't going to release any of my records, so we pestered Dick Leahy at least to fix up a promotion trip for us, just to introduce the Americans to Glitter. Utall saw the wisdom in this, because anything that raised my profile without actually putting out any records would further strengthen his hand; so in April 1974 we set off to spend five weeks travelling across America, creating as many media opportunities as possible. Mike was quite cool about the whole thing – he'd been to the States a lot when he worked with Bert Burns – but it was my first time there and I was really excited.

Things began to go wrong, though, the moment we touched down in Los Angeles. I was wearing the full Glitter gear, as usual; I think I had a fur coat, too, as it was still cold when we left England. The US customs officials took one look at me and carted me off to a side room. They spent an hour looking for drugs, and they *really* looked, because I felt absolutely used and abused afterwards – the stupid thing was that only a complete idiot would bring illegal substances *into* Los Angeles, because everything you could want is available there twenty-four hours a day. When the strip search was over they took my shoes to be specially X-rayed because they'd never seen platform soles before; even though Elton had broken big in America by then, he was still wearing T-shirts. I thought that was particularly daft, as it would have been such an obvious hiding place, but I kept my mouth shut as the officials seemed to have the right to do what they liked with me.

The tour was organised by Gibson-Stromberg, which was considered the most innovative PR firm of the time – it was they who had designed the Rolling Stones' tongue logo – but they were wildly off base with their ideas for me. I stayed in a bungalow in the grounds of the Beverly Hills Hotel and my first engagement was to meet the press, or rather not to meet the press. Newspapers, magazines, TV crews and photographers had been invited to a very swanky buffet lunch, and I was supposed to change costumes every twenty minutes – the excess baggage charge on what we'd brought out had run into thousands – and parade round the swimming pool. I was to play the role an eccentric Englishman – I presume the theme was mad dogs and Englishmen out in the noon-day sun – and if a reporter tried to speak to me I had to be rude to them: barking about how I couldn't get a decent cup of tea, or complaining that nobody in the hotel could understand the Queen's English. I went along with the idea because Gibson-Stromberg were supposed to know what they were doing, but I didn't like it at all because it wasn't me – I did my best PR when I just sat down and had a chat, but that was the last thing they wanted.

Then every evening between five and seven I'd have to go and sit in the Polo Lounge at the hotel, which was apparently where everybody important in the entertainment industry went for cocktails. It was the place to be seen in, so I had to have the best table – I dread to think how many thousand dollars they had to bung the Maître d' – wear a different costume each evening and, as before, be rude to people. But nobody took any notice, because all the other customers were seasoned showbiz folk and had seen it all before. The only interesting thing that happened was one evening when I arrived to find Elizabeth Taylor sitting at my table. I assumed it had been bought and paid for on my behalf and pointed out to her that she was in my seat. She replied, very regally, 'Are you sure?' and gave me such a sexy smile that I fell apart and just mumbled, 'No, not really' and walked off!

The other PR plan was to have a party in every

major city on the tour, to which would be invited various off-beat American celebrities – the intention was that I should be seen entertaining my fellow eccentrics. In reality, though, it was just a ruse to make sure I was photographed with as many well-known faces as possible since the *real* big stars – the A-list celebrities – would never have turned up to be seen with a far-from-famous Brit. The ballroom at the hotel was hired for the LA event, and a regular rent-a-crowd were invited, plus some kids from LA's only glam disco and characters such as Dustin Hoffman, Alan Price, Alice Cooper and a guy called Cal Worthington – a used-car dealer who had become a celebrity through appearing in the TV adverts for his showroom.

In the afternoon Alice Cooper, whom I knew from *Top of the Pops*, phoned me and told me he was bringing a surprise to the party. I figured he meant a snake and took no notice, but he turned up with a snake and Groucho Marx! It was wonderful. The whole place went silent and stood to applaud when Groucho walked in; this wasn't long before he died and he was practically senile, so he never went out. He and Alice were good friends, for reasons that are completely beyond me; he'd persuaded Groucho to come, and then sat him next to me. I'm a huge Marx Brothers fan and could hardly believe I was sitting next to Groucho. When I first started talking to him, however, he was so gaga I got no response at all. Suddenly, though, he came out of it and turned into the liveliest person I'd ever met; he was hilarious. He took the mickey out of everybody in the room and rattled off patter so quickly I couldn't keep up. But when the press wanted a shot of me with my arm round his shoulders – the typical showbiz all-mates-together picture – he wouldn't play. Just as abruptly as he'd come to life he relapsed, and by now the photographers were desperate for their picture. The girl Groucho had with him – she was a nurse-cum-secretary – said she knew how to make him smile: she undid her blouse, took out one of her more than ample boobs and put the nipple in her mouth. Slowly, Groucho began to smile and I was pushed in next to him for the picture.

After the party, I was pretty gone and invited dozens of people back to my bungalow to continue. Unfortunately things got very out of hand: there was a crowd from earlier in the evening, friends of friends of friends, and an assortment of hookers and down-town lowlife that somehow got wind of it. Everybody began ordering champagne, lobster and anything else they fancied on my room account, and it got so noisy that first of all the police arrived to ask if we could keep it down, and then the manager threatened to throw me out unless it stopped immediately. I probably would have argued with him, but I was sidetracked by Alan Price who had climbed on a table and started to yell at people in his Geordie accent. During that period he was pretty dissatisfied because he believed the industry had treated him badly, and it was as if all his discontentment bubbled to the surface that night. He unleashed one of the worst torrents of abuse I've ever heard – he was yelling at the crowd: 'Fuck off, the lot of you! Get out now! You're nothing but leeches!' Then he started imploring me to get rid of everybody, because they'd bleed me dry then throw me aside. I tried to calm him down, but he started physically pushing people out and offering to fight anybody who fancied it. It cleared the room in about five minutes, but not before Dustin Hoffman had squared up to me. He was pretty well out of it, and had convinced himself I was making a play for the lady he was with, and then used the mayhem Alan had started to have a go at me.

We left Los Angeles two days after that. We'd been there two weeks, and from a PR point of view it was a disaster: we'd spent a fortune – the sum of $250,000 was mentioned, and at the time I didn't realise it came out of my royalties; and for that all the press coverage we got was either of Groucho Marx being seen in public or a few articles which pretty much said: 'This man may be the biggest thing in Europe, but we couldn't get a word of sense out of him. We don't know what it is he does and he did nothing to help us find out.' The trip was then shortened to take in just Chicago and New York. But Mike was so fed up by then that he didn't go to Chicago; he stayed in LA to get a bit of rest, and met me later in New York.

I felt the pressure was off me slightly when I arrived in Chicago, so I was determined to enjoy myself. I went to meet a lot of the radio jocks who had originally played the record, and they were really nice. A few of them got quite a shock when they met me: the records had come out only in paper sleeves and they thought I was black, until I walked in wearing all the Glitter gear. I had a party and the Chicago Bear grid-iron football team turned up – they were all about twice the size of me and thought it was hilarious. I was there for nearly a week, and Gibson-Stromberg laid on anything I wanted to keep me happy – if I wanted a girl, there was a girl; if I wanted two, there were two. But they got very worried when

I had a night off and said I wanted to go and see Bill Withers, who was playing at a club in town. They told me it wouldn't be cool because it was a black club, and they wouldn't take me. After getting on so well with the black radio DJs I wasn't going to let that stop me, so I went with my assistant Douglas, a very dapper Englishman who always wore a pinstripe suit and had bright red hair. On tour we worked out a butler routine for him: he would hover behind me, dusting my chair off before I sat down and fetching me things while I, in my best upper-crust voice, screamed phrases like 'I say, chappie!' – it used to crack the Americans up.

When we arrived the club was nearly empty and I can remember thinking what a dump it was for somebody like Bill Withers to be playing in. We sat by the stage and waited, and as it filled up we began to realise we were the only white people in the place: we started to get some very funny looks – I was in Glitter gear as I had no other clothes with me. The show was brilliant, but afterwards a fairly young guy approached me and asked me, quite threateningly, what we were doing there because we weren't black. I was fairly frightened but figured silliness was the best form of defence, so I looked down at myself and, in a very English accent, said 'What do you mean, I'm not black? What are you, colour blind?' He stared at me for a few seconds and then broke into laughter! We got on very well after that and I stayed to get rather drunk with him and his friends. It was just one of those situations where people seldom exposed to the other side of the fence end up with all the wrong ideas. It's sad, really, but so prevalent. As Gary Glitter I always worked to pull the fence down, and at times like that I got through.

When I got to New York I began to get very depressed. It was my thirtieth birthday and I was missing my family and friends at home, with whom I would usually have celebrated. Thirty is so often a time when people take stock, and I was beginning to resent the attitude of the music press in the UK who at every opportunity sneered at me – it was starting to get through. This trip wasn't very fulfilling, either – in fact now I could see how it had run out of Mike's and my control. I began to wonder if I was starting to crack and how long I'd be able to keep it up. I'd never thought like that before. That evening I was waiting to go on the *Wolfman Jack* radio show and was feeling very subdued. Things weren't made any easier by the guest before me, who was Ian Hunter from Mott the Hoople. He'd auditioned for me as a bass player years before; now he was acting the superstar in New York and wouldn't talk to me. Before I went on air the Wolfman couldn't understand why I was quiet when my records were so outrageous – he kept offering me things to get me up: 'Wanna toot? Wanna smoke? Wanna drink?' Eventually I asked him for a gin and tonic, and then as soon as I was on started to shout and act wild. The Wolfman was completely stunned and told his listeners: 'All this man's had is gin and tonic! For God's sake, bring me some gin and tonic!'

We were on air for about two hours and had a really good time fooling about and playing records, but as soon as I got back in the car I felt sad again. I think at that point I could easily have packed it in, but when I arrived back at my suite in the hotel all of Led Zeppelin, their manager Peter Grant, and Maggie Bell were waiting with a huge cake and a crate of champagne. I cried my eyes out.

It really picked me up, and once we'd cut the cake John Bonham took me downstairs, saying he had something to show me. We went into the bar and he produced a big pair of tailor's shears. Looking like Harpo Marx and with a mad smile on his face he walked up to all the Madison Avenue executive types and began snipping their ties off just below the knots! I was stunned, but nobody batted an eyelid; when he'd gone all round the bar he put the shears and the tie ends into his pocket and we went back upstairs. It was bizarre. After that we all went to a transvestite club – remember, we were very out of it – and it got raided by the police. Led Zeppelin were very sure they didn't want to be up in front of a judge for being caught in there, so got out by climbing through a window in the ladies' loo. I had a bit of difficulty because I wasn't nearly as skinny as the rest of them, and Robert Plant risked getting caught to hang around and help me through.

It was a fantastic night – exactly what I needed. I can remember thinking: so what if a few journalists rubbish me? Here I am with some of the biggest names in rock doing their best to give me a good time. It was like an incident a year later in Australia when I went to a David Bowie show. None of the journalists who had lionised him was given access; I was the only person allowed in the dressing room, and afterwards we went out on the town. It was acceptance from people like him that made all the difference.

I didn't return to America for over a year, by which time Larry Utall had sold out to Columbia and they'd given the label to Clive Davis to run as Arista

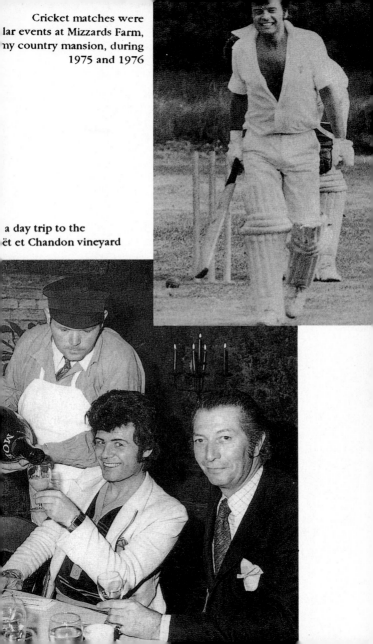

Cricket matches were
lar events at Mizzards Farm,
ny country mansion, during
1975 and 1976

a day trip to the
ët et Chandon vineyard

The Farewell Tour, 1976.
Mike Leander models
the robes backstage...
(David Magnus)

GOODBYE

...I say my good
(David Mag

Gary Glitter's
Rock'n'Roll Circus
in 1981

A publicity picture
for the mid 80s
university shows

Back as the Leader
in 1987 (Lewis Ziolex)

In the kids' TV drama
How to be Cool in 1988
(Granada TV)

With Mum...

...and Alison

In the recording studio in 1990. Left to right: Jef Hanlon, my son Paul, and the Gang Show bandleader Mark Pearson (Colin Levy)

In training for the Gang Show (*Daily Mirror*)

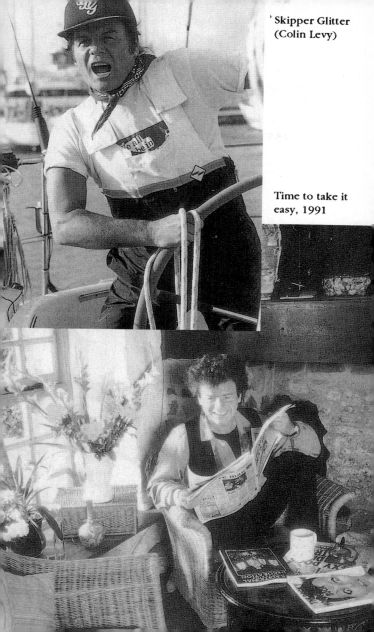

Skipper Glitter
(Colin Levy)

Time to take it
easy, 1991

With the Gang (Steve Wright)

Records. It was his idea that I went to New York to record the *GG* album. Clive Davis had made his name at Columbia by discovering Simon and Garfunkel and Barry Manilow and had picked up the option on my contract certain that my music would never sell in America unless he personally oversaw my career there. He didn't seem to take account of the fact that, without his help, I was the hottest act in Europe and Australia and every record I had put out so far in the USA had been a hit.

Davis had just acted as executive producer on 'It's in His Kiss' by Linda Lewis. As one of the first true disco records it had been a hit on both sides of the Atlantic, and he insisted that I make the album with the two guys who produced that single, Tony Silvester and Bert DeCoteaux. Ray Brown struck the deal for me to do it, as he was unhappy with Mike being writer, producer and manager and, as he saw it, creaming it off in all directions. So we allowed ourselves to be led – we were both desperate to get into the American market, and everybody at the UK record company told us how flattering it was that the great Clive Davis was taking such a personal interest in my career. We flew out for a three-week recording session in May 1975, but I wasn't at all sure about the situation; Mike was even less so.

When we came through immigration at Kennedy Airport there was no limousine waiting for us and nobody from the record company in sight. After two years of getting VIP treatment everywhere else we couldn't believe it. We took a cab to the hotel where Mike, who was much more of a prima donna than I was, got on the phone and started to shout at the record company. They were very laid back about it, and the only person he got to speak to was a secretary who said she thought we might want to sleep after the journey. At that point Mike exploded and demanded to speak to Clive Davis immediately, saying that unless he called us personally within the next hour we were going back to London. He didn't, so we did. I was stunned, I'd just finished unpacking when I had to put it all back and get in a cab to the airport. On the plane on the way back we met Dick Leahy, who didn't seem too bothered about the incident. We played pontoon with him and I lost £500. A bit dazed by the events of the past few hours I began drinking steadily, and got so pissed that even I shudder to think about it: I had to be taken off the plane in a wheelchair!

It was early in the morning UK time when we arrived back, but it seemed as if half our record company was waiting for us. While I sat in a lounge with people trying to sober me up the executives pleaded with us to go back, saying they'd all get the sack if we didn't. Mike flatly refused, but Ray said I had to so I was put back on a plane to New York by myself. When I arrived, the biggest limousine I'd ever seen had been sent to meet me and Clive Davis was waiting at the hotel. He'd taken us at our word when Mike had told him how precious my time was: the sessions started that night and were booked solid for three weeks. That's when I discovered cocaine – the only way I could keep up the non-stop schedule was to dig into it and keep on going. I only slept once – straight through the only weekend I had off – the entire time I was there.

I had one night off, too, and that was anything other than restful. The record company had phoned me to tell me that Paul Rogers of Bad Company was in town and coming down to see me, but warned me to be careful of him because he liked to fight. Paul dropped into the studio and was fine, and invited me to the band's big Chinese meal after their Madison Square Garden show the next night. After the meal the plan was to go to Ashley's, the then trendy New York club. I was getting in my limousine – it was at my disposal for the entire time I was there – when I saw Paul and the girl who was with him looking for a car. I couldn't believe the man who had just played Madison Square Gardens hadn't had a car sent for him, so I offered them a lift along with Maggie Bell, Hamish Stuart and another member of the Average White Band who was already in my limo.

Everybody seemed to be getting on very well until Paul, obviously spoiling for a fight, said to Hamish, 'I think the Average White Band are very fucking average!' There was a deathly hush until the other guy from the Average White Band made a not very kind remark about Paul's girlfriend, at which Paul leaned over, took the guy's glasses off his face and threw them out of the sunroof. I was laughing very falsely and trying to turn it all into a joke, when Hamish took Paul's girlfriend's hat and threw it out of the roof, too. That was it. Paul flew at him while the other chap jumped on Paul. Maggie and the other girl just lay on the floor screaming at the top of their lungs – and Maggie Bell has got some lungs! At that point the driver, a big guy who doubled as my security, pulled over and threw them all out. From the pavement it must have looked hilarious. The car rocking, the screams and sounds of a fight coming through the roof, and then a huge black guy leaping out, opening the door and hauling out some very famous rock stars! The interior of the limousine looked like a war zone – the cocktail cabinet, the phone and the television were all wrecked and I ended up with a bill for $20,000. I wish I'd been able to video it – I would have got all of that back!

The actual sessions were quite an experience for me. Everybody was black except the drummer and me, the then unknown Luther Vandross was one of the background singers, while Kool and the Gang were in the next studio and Aretha Franklin was down the corridor. There was a totally different attitude than in Britain. It was much looser: everybody dropped in to contribute to each other's sessions; everybody's point of view counted for something – if one of the string players had an idea for a bass line, they were listened to; and nothing was so perfect it couldn't be improved. Once I got used to this approach I relaxed completely and Bert coaxed out of me some soul singing that was far superior to anything I had done in Germany – Tony Silvester, the other half of the production team, was hardly ever there. But somewhere along the line Gary Glitter got lost and Paul Raven re-emerged. When I got back and played the tapes to Mike he said it was a very good album, but it wasn't Glitter. It was a curious hybrid of R&B and New York disco, and far too polished for my audience. The single from it, 'Papa Oom Mow Mow', only got to Number 38 in the UK, which was my poorest showing as Gary Glitter; and the album only sold twenty thousand over here.

Arista in the USA never even released it, and I heard much later that the option on my contract had only been picked up because the company was selling its European distribution rights to EMI, from Polygram, and I was part of the deal. That switch also undermined my status in Europe, as we'd spent three years building up relationships with Polygram's Continental network and now we had to start again. We'd been stuffed, and my chance of success in America was gone for another few years.

8
Life Is Not A Dress Rehearsal

By the end of 1973, after a year of success I was starting to feel a bit cut off by my fame. I didn't socialise with the Glitterband much, because the band mentality is very different from a singer's: theirs is much more of an all-lads-together attitude. Vocalists are immediately set apart because they can't join in the musicians' conversations, and will very often – as was my case – be the band's employer. I didn't socialise with other solo artists at that time, either. This was largely due to nervousness on my part. I'd become so successful so quickly that I was still in awe of those who had been up there for a while, and would never make the first move to talk to them. I've since found out that many other stars felt the same way, and although they always appeared aloof it wasn't out of snobbishness but because they were intimidated by those who were actually their peers. I only went to the BBC bar after *Top of the Pops* once, after my first appearance, and that was because I wanted to see David Bowie who'd been performing 'Space Oddity'. When I got there he held his court and I held mine, and so all we did was nod to each other.

The TV programmes where several bands appeared were obviously the occasions on which we came into contact with each other most frequently. The public may have thought that all the artists larked about together off set, but that couldn't actually be further from the truth. Different acts had staggered schedules for wardrobe, rehearsals, breaks and performance, and although there was always a lot of hanging about – an act could be at the studios for anything up to six hours – frontmen such as myself would have to do interviews and photo sessions during the breaks. It was the bands which played behind us that did all the socialising, because they didn't have the same demands on them. Their day would involve a great deal of hanging about, during which they'd drop in on each other's dressing rooms. The Glitterband met many more performers than I ever did. Slade was often on the same *Top of the Pops* as I was, yet because Noddy Holder and I both had huge extra-circular workloads we didn't actually meet for ages.

At that time I couldn't go anywhere without attracting attention, either. I was living in a service flat in Troy Court, just off Kensington High Street, and on rare days off I felt forced to stay at home. This wasn't a relaxing situation, because at any time of day there would be a couple of hundred fans outside the block; as a result I didn't even feel safe looking out of the window. The contrast between the weeks of frantic activity that made up most of my life and then living like a virtual hermit always threw me off balance a bit, and emphasised the problems of coming to terms with my fame. At times I would feel so pent up I'd begin to wonder what I was doing it all for.

It was Keith Moon who snapped me out of it. I

knew him vaguely, but I wouldn't have thought of him as a friend; then one evening he bribed his way past the porter downstairs and, completely unannounced, knocked on my door with two of the girls from outside in tow. The girls were so excited they practically had to hold each other up, but Keith just grinned at me and said, 'Can I borrow your bedroom?' Then he disappeared in there with them. He did this on several successive nights. I thought it was unfair to take advantage of the fans, and told him not to do it any more. His reply was that he didn't think it was right *he* took advantage of them when I wasn't, and said that my wasting them should be a criminal offence. The next time he called round he shoved a girl into my bedroom and just pushed me in after her! I think that was when my outlook on success altered.

Keith was a lovely man. He was a bit barmy and absolutely out of it all the time, but he was determined to enjoy his success. He came from a whole generation of groups that thought that way – the Faces, the Stones, Led Zeppelin and so on, all had the same attitude and were the last wave of pop stars to admit the only reason they formed bands was that it was the best way to get free drinks and get laid. Keith's attitude to fame was, 'Why are you working so hard for it if you're not going to have a bit of fun with it when you get it?' As he was very fond of telling me, life isn't a dress rehearsal.

He convinced me to get off my backside and go out, then made sure I made the most of every available minute by showing me where and how. He introduced me to a circuit of places where having a famous face would get you in and then make sure you had a good time, usually with somebody else footing the bill: we'd go to clubs, restaurants and every celebrity party on offer, where we'd get very wrecked and generally behave like we thought pop stars should! I think the reason he and I got on so well was that there was quite a bit of the Keith Moon spirit in me, just waiting for someone to bring it out.

But associating with him also became a bit of a liability, as he used to sleep less than I did. Some nights I'd be so exhausted all I wanted to do was stay in bed by myself, but Keith would call at about 2 a.m. wanting to hit the town. I'd try to ignore his thumping on the door, but he'd tear up strips of newspaper, light one end and poke them through the letterbox – his plan was to smoke me out! It always got me up, too, but on several occasions started a small fire. I had to buy quite a few new front doors.

In 1974, Rod Stewart got me out of another very difficult patch. I knew Rod through going out with Keith – he'd had a lot of money for quite a bit longer, so had had more time to come to terms with the way it had changed his life. I think he could see that I was beginning to burn myself out once Keith showed me how to enjoy life as a pop star. He rang me up one evening, and over dinner invited me to come down and stay at his house in the country for a couple of days. I didn't really want to, but he insisted it would do me good, so I tagged along. We got back to his house near Ascot at about 4 a.m., both fairly drunk, and then spent a good hour in his living room singing 'Land of Hope and Glory' in loud tenor voices – I'm not quite sure why. When he showed me round the place I was immediately impressed – it had all the pop star trappings: pool, big fireplaces and paintings everywhere. His bedroom was the funniest place: it was completely decked out in Scottish flags! His eiderdown cover was a huge flag, he had one hanging from the ceiling over the bed, they were on the walls, draped over chairs – I've never seen so many. It particularly made me chuckle because we'd just spent the past hour singing a true blue English song.

I stayed over, and the next day he said, 'Come on, let's go down the pub.' I was stunned – I hadn't done anything like that for nearly two years! When we got to his local in the village, he just introduced me as his mate Gary and we got on with having a drink like everybody else in there. He said he thought it was absolutely essential for somebody in my position to go on living as normally as possible, and that the only way I could hope to do that was to get out of London and away from the press, the fans and the night life. All of that would still be there if I wanted to go and live it up, but I had to be able to balance it by dropping into some funny little pub like this where nobody would take a blind bit of notice of me.

I looked around at the other guys in the bar and realised how right he was – they had lived and worked in that village all their lives, and didn't care how many hits Rod had had. As long as he didn't act flash they treated him normally, and had accepted him into their community. For a long time I'd imagined that as soon as anyone made it they had to live in London because that was the centre of the British music business, but my life in the capital had become completely removed from reality – I was either working, out on the town or hiding from fans. At that point I understood why so many successful pop stars move to the country, and Rod showed me it was possible to be famous and live comfortably as well.

I enjoyed the high life with Rod, too. At the time he was just splitting up with Dee Harrington, the lady before Britt Ekland, so he was on the prowl; I think he saw my flat in Kensington as somewhere to take women to. I wasn't too worried about that, though, as I was quite happy to go out on the prowl with him. We did very well in the ladies' stakes at my flat – including members of the Guinness family, who were regular visitors – until Rod met Britt. Rod was brilliant to hang out with – he wasn't as volatile as Keith Moon, but he's actually the funniest man I know. He tends not to let the outside world see this, but among his friends nearly everything Rod says is achingly funny. He's got a wickedly sharp wit when it comes to sending up people or things, and I'm certain he would have been a stand-up comedian if he hadn't become a singer.

He was also one of the very few people who understood completely what life was like for me, because he was just as famous and had been for longer. It was strange, but when we were out together it was as if we stole the limelight from each other, so the fans never made as much fuss as if we'd been separate. There were obviously a lot of places we couldn't go, though, and one of those was the Speakeasy. This really surprised me, because for years the place had been a rock star hang-out, and in the early seventies it was to *Top of the Pops* what Ad Lib had been to *Ready Steady Go* ten years previously – the official after-show watering-hole. All the bands, like Mud, Slade, the Sweet and the Glitterband, used to hang out down there, but the night Rod and I walked in it went completely silent – it was obvious we weren't meant to be there. The place had become a club for bands, not singers, for musicians rather than celebrities, and although Rod hadn't split from the Faces by then we were just that little bit bigger as individuals. That night the atmosphere felt as if the prefects had tried to join in with the fun behind the bike sheds, and it made everybody feel uneasy. We never went back, and started hanging out at Tramp where we felt much more relaxed.

Tramp was like a club in the true sense of the word: either your wealth or your very famous face was your membership card. They were very strict about who they let in – the clientele were Arabs and younger members of the aristocracy, and the only celebrities were in the mega-league: the Stones, Keith Moon, Jeff Beck, Michael Caine, Eric Clapton occasionally, George Best and a few other footballers and, later on, John Conteh. The good thing about keeping admission so exclusive was that it removed the stigma, because we were all as famous as each other and could relax and chat to each other easily.

Tramp had two other features that were attractive to my lifestyle. Where there's a lot of money you'll always find the best-looking women; and although the official door policy was to admit couples only, some of the most stunning women in London managed to get in unescorted. The size of the cubicles in the toilets was a bonus too: they've been changed now, but in those days they were so large they'd comfortably accommodate a private party of half a dozen people sharing a line of coke or each other's bodies. Nobody ever did any drugs in the club, so people would disappear into the loo in a way that wasn't exactly blatant but was still very obvious. I know the owner, Johnny Gold, has cleaned the place up now;

he either genuinely didn't know what was going on then or he turned a very convincing blind eye.

The only time I've ever really had anything to do with Mick Jagger was through Tramp when, at the end of 1974, he took Keith Moon, Kit Lambert, Keith Richards and myself back to his house in Cheyne Walk, Chelsea. Jagger had heard I knew a bit about wine, so he took me down to his cellar and showed me round his very extensive and valuable collection, talking at great length about different vintages and regions. Admittedly I didn't know much about Jagger as a person, but it really surprised me how expert he was on wine. We then went upstairs, where he made everybody sit down and listen to these obscure reggae records he'd brought back from Jamaica – he kept asking the assembled company if anybody had ever heard this track or that track, which of course nobody had. Again, he was an expert and started explaining to me what was going on inside the rhythms and commenting on little subtleties of the mix. Once more I was impressed, and by then very flattered that he chose to talk to me about this – that was until I noticed that everyone else was out of it and I was the only one listening!

What really shocked me later that night was Ronnie Wood showing up. I knew Ronnie because he and I had briefly shared a squat in Shepherds Bush in the sixties, but I also knew that Ronnie was in Rod Stewart's band the Faces and that Rod and Jagger were sworn enemies. I sat quietly listening to the conversations and discovered that Jagger was poaching Ronnie to joint the Stones! He'd decided, for reasons I've never found out, that the band's next guitarist had to be from London and Ronnie fitted the bill, so the offer had been made and Jagger was just sorting out the details before he nicked him from Rod. Not surprisingly, given my friendship with his current employer, Ronnie looked very worried from the moment he saw me. At every opportunity he'd pull me into a corner and whisper, 'Don't tell Rod! Don't tell Rod! It's too early!'

Tramp was the middle ground in three levels of London night life: the Speakeasy, Tramp and Annabel's. Annabel's was for the gentry – it was very snooty, and you needed both a tie and a title to get in there. A lot of the aristocracy were into rock music, though, and used to come down to Tramp for a bit of excitement, knowing they could rub shoulders with the upper-bracket rock stars who had left the Speakeasy to get away from the rabble. The irony was that this was just about the time that the aristocracy started running out of money, while the rock stars were earning fortunes and buying up the stately homes that the impoverished gentry were putting on the market! We actually felt we had become the new aristocracy, yet to the outside world it was the titled folk who had all the class and we were just jumped-up working-class oiks. Both sides got on very well together, though, and one of the best days of my life was spent with a bunch of young dukes and earls.

Willy Robertson, an insurance broker for the major rock tours, organised a charity trip to the Moët et Chandon vineyards in France for a party of about thirty people, including George Morton – who owns most of Lincolnshire – Patrick Lichfield, the Earl of Denby, Keith Emerson and me. We met for an 8 a.m. champagne breakfast at London Airport, then boarded a private plane to fly to an army base somewhere in France – I say 'somewhere in France', because by the time we got there everybody was so wrecked that nobody was sure exactly where. It was only about 10.30 by then, but after the reception and what was served on the flight we'd already drunk enough champagne to swim in – it wouldn't have surprised me if the plane had been fuelled on it too! We were taken to the château by coach, by which time the trip had degenerated into a real lads' outing, a beano for lager louts who could afford champagne – Keith and I had to stop the coach to have a pee in a field, while thirty-odd members of the British ruling class jeered at us out of the windows!

When we arrived at this magnificent château, for some reason I was treated like the guest of honour: at lunch I was seated next to the count who owned the château. But first we were taken on a tour of the champagne vaults, which consisted of twenty-five miles of tunnels lined with racks of bottles. We went round on an open electric train – much like several large golf carts coupled together – and as we travelled people were standing up, pulling out bottles and spraying them over each other. Then those of us from the music circle lit up some joints. I'm not a great smoker, but as I was in this gang for the day I had a few puffs. It had been laced with LSD, and I had a terrifying trip – I've been told that at one point I stood at the bottom of the long staircase leading up from the cellars unable to climb it because every time I lifted my foot I saw my leg extend to the very top step.

It wore off by lunchtime, and when we sat down to eat in a special room in the vaults everybody was a little subdued – by then we'd been drinking non-top for seven hours. But we were served a 1918 champagne, which was fairly potent, and after we'd drunk the toast with it the mood definitely went up a notch. Then the count made a speech and brought out a 1911 champagne. This was why lunch had been served in this particular room, which was pressurised: if these ancient bottles had been taken outside they would have exploded. The 1911 champagne was what I'd imagine nectar to taste like – it had very little fizz in it, and was much sweeter than I would have expected champagne to be. But it had such a kick and everybody went wally – we started shouting, throwing any leftover food about and smashing crockery!

We went back up to the château after that, where there was an auction for a Methuselah of champagne – it holds the equivalent of eight bottles. I ended up with it after bidding £500, which is remarkable considering I was in the company of some of the richest men in the country. Then we were each given a hamper containing bottles of champagne and after-shave lotion and left to get the plane home. It was a good thing my Methuselah was sent home separately, otherwise it would never have arrived: as soon as the plane took off we drank all the champagne in our hampers and by then were so pissed we drank the aftershave! I don't even remember getting off the plane! I may have been wheeled off on a stretcher – in fact I think most of us must have been! It was a magical day.

Late in the summer of 1975 I took Rod's advice and moved to the country. I bought Mizzards Farm, a large house with twelve acres of land in Hampshire. I paid £70,000 for it, which was a very good price, but I spent a further £100,000 on renovations and repairs.

It needed a whole new plumbing system, which involved getting water piped in from the road across four fields. I had a pool and large patio area put in – the pool I kept heated all through the winter, and although it had an insulated cover on it, if I drove past on a frosty morning I could see steam coming off it. I spent £25,000 on the kitchen – more than most houses cost in 1974 – but it had a huge oven that was custom-made in Birmingham, and one of the first domestic microwaves in the country. Then, as I didn't like the front door where it was, I had it bricked up in very expensive antique Sussex stone; but I never got round to having the new one put in, so anybody who called had to come in through the kitchen.

The interior was quite spectacular. There was a huge dining room, with a thirty-foot ceiling and galleries running round it on two floors that led to ten bedrooms. The living room was about forty feet square with a massive fireplace and a study leading off it. Past that was the east wing. It contained four rooms which I had fitted out like a luxury hotel suite, because by then that was the only kind of living arrangement with which I could identify. My suite consisted of a living room with a log fireplace, huge couches and subdued lighting – a bachelor play room. There was a secret room that could only be entered through a false wall in my bedroom. In there I kept my clothes, any cash I might have, important papers and various illegal substances. The bathroom cost me a small fortune – it featured gold taps and an octagonal bath, made from imported Italian marble that was so big I often had six people in there with me. Then there was my bedroom, which became quite a talking point in my bankruptcy hearing several years later. It had hand-made silk curtains operated by electric motors, which could be either remote-controlled or set on a light-sensitive switch, and cost £6,000. The bed was bigger than king-size and octagonal, with eight posts and a canopy. There were remote-controlled lights set into panels all round the room, and next to the bed was a fridge with a machine built in that poured and handed out a glass of champagne every time the door was opened. On a few occasions the electrics in my bedroom went completely haywire, as if the gremlins had got into the system: the lights would turn on and off by themselves, the curtains wouldn't stop opening and closing and the champagne dispenser was pouring bubbly out inside the fridge – I felt like a bit-part player in the Peter Sellers film *The Party*!

In between the east wing and the kitchen, though, the house had nothing in it at all. The only other rooms I ever furnished were the breakfast room and the kitchen – which probably never had any food in the fridge – because after buying the house and paying for what I'd bought already, I didn't have enough money to buy the fine antique furniture I wanted, and I didn't have time to choose it anyway. Although it must have looked strange to visitors as they walked from a very luxurious kitchen through a completely bare house to my opulent living quarters, the only time this ever bothered me was the Christmas after I'd moved in. I really fancied a big family Christmas like we used to have at 36 South Barr, so I invited all my relatives and several friends from London to come and stay. I knew I had to furnish the whole place, instantly, so I got the RAM office to contact the BBC props department and hire a stately home's worth of antique furniture for Christmas week. The props people were the one department who were helpful when we asked for things to use on *Top of the Pops*, and they said they'd see what they could do: three days later a convoy of BBC lorries pulled up and the entire set from the drama series *The Duchess of Duke Street* was delivered. The furniture looked fantastic – huge mahogany sideboards, lovely tables and beautifully carved chairs – but none of the carpets fitted properly, so the magnificent Persian rugs were either folded up at the edges or a few feet of bare board was visible! I didn't tell my family where I got it from, and they were greatly impressed. The bill, however, was astronomical: I was to be charged £4,000 for the week, but as I quite liked the stuff I didn't send it back until the middle of February – it would have been far cheaper to buy its equivalent, and that way I could have made sure the carpets fitted!

I took on two permanent gardeners and a housekeeper who came in every day, the swimming pool was completed, and then I settled down to enjoy the end of the summer. I'd never owned any house before, so that in itself was a great thrill, but having such a grand country home really made me feel like the lord of the manor. I was eager to play the role to the full, and as cricket was part of the village way of life I started my own team made up of friends and people from the music business. I'm actually much more of a soccer fan – it was Mike who followed cricket – but the idea of balmy summer afternoons and the sound of leather on willow fitted in exactly with my country squire pose. The problem was we had nowhere to play, as the local recreation ground at Rogate was fine for football but completely unsuitable for cricket. Undaunted, I went to a garden centre, bought an entire cricket pitch worth of prime turf, had the ground levelled and put it down. It cost me several thousand pounds, but it was a pitch the MCC would have been proud of. The regular village side used it for their games, while my team would play on it against Chrysalis Records, Tim Rice's XI and other music business teams. My squad was always fairly flexible: Mike, Eddie Seago and sixties pop star Jess Conrad played in most matches, but otherwise it included any performers or managers who fancied a game. Sometimes we'd even get a few of Middlesex's junior players down: they wanted to hang out with pop stars; and we always wanted to beat Chrysalis, who took it very seriously. By the end of the following summer we actually got quite good and went to play a few away games.

The matches would go on all over the weekend, when Mizzards Farm would look like a hippie commune: because I had twelve acres of land but only two or three beds in my house the players and their friends would come down in motor homes or would pitch tents. I always laid on hospitality and would do a barbecue by the pool, for which a standard order from the butchers would be two hundred lamb chops, two hundred pork chops and two hundred steaks. I had a running tab at the local pub while we were playing, too, and I'd provide crates of champagne for the party afterwards. That's what those weekends were really – forty-eight-hour parties which happened to involve a game of cricket.

Of course a good deal of silliness went on, too: a game we'd usually play in the early hours of Sunday morning involved getting into teams of about three or

four people and carrying out commando raids on the
occupied bedrooms or the people staying in the
grounds. The idea was to catch people either not
looking cool – dishevelled hair or no make-up – or to
burst in on them when they were in what might be
called 'a compromising position'. It was quite well
organised, with a carefully thought-out scale of points
for catching different people in different situations, so
we took it seriously and would crawl around on our
stomachs, sometimes with bits of twig in our hair and
dirt on our faces. The highest score was to catch Jess
Conrad with his hair looking messy, because Jess was
one of the old showbiz characters who never let
anybody see him looking less than immaculate. All
summer we tried to catch him, but every time a squad
burst in on him he'd be sitting on the end of his bed
wearing perfectly pressed pyjamas with not a hair out
of place.

We'd have a lot of fun after the games, when the
team would all use my bathroom and jump into the
huge tub like a football team to create a real all-lads-
together locker room situation. One day Billy Ocean
came down to play – he was an excellent cricketer, but
nobody really knew him so he was a little shy. When
he came into the bathroom after the game he was the
only guy in there with a towel wrapped round his
waist. Straightaway people started geeing him about
how black guys were supposed to be better endowed,
and jeering that he must have been overlooked if he
was so ashamed he had to cover it up – all very grown-
up stuff. Then he dropped his towel and our words
went straight back down our throats – it practically
hung down to his knees!

I was living the way I believed a successful pop star

should. I realised Gary Glitter was bigger than Paul Gadd could ever hope to be, and people wanted to know me. I knew a great deal of that had come about just because I was famous, but I figured that as long as they were good fun it didn't matter – Rod was like that, too: he had a very camp entourage who were really only there because they made him laugh. During my time at Mizzards Farm I wanted to party as much as anybody else did, and the fact that I was picking up the tab seemed incidental. On reflection, I believe that because my good fortune had come after years of trying I knew how hard it was to make it, and so I was willing to share it with people who hadn't done as well as I had. I believe I was doing exactly what I hadn't done in my teenage years, too – a kind of belated post-adolescence. I always have been a bit of a lad, but when I was nineteen and twenty I never got the chance to do the things that guys of that age usually get up to: have a game of football, enjoy a bit of a drink and chase the women. Rod was much the same in this respect, too, and this was perfectly illustrated by the Sunday football matches we played in late 1974 and early 1975. He used to take me down to the house of a friend of his, Ronnie Shaw, a very wealthy businessman who lived behind the Brands Hatch racetrack in Kent. Ronnie had his own private football pitch – floodlights, a small stand, everything – and it was his own team we'd turn out for; Elton played once or twice, too. It was great fun: I was too lazy to run about too much so I would goal hang and Rod, who is a very good footballer, would knock the ball over to me all the time – quite often I'd slip one in! Then there was all the post-match mickey-taking and arguing in the changing rooms, after which we'd go back to the house for a few drinks and try and interfere with the girls lying around the pool. We were following exactly the same guidelines as any lad in his early twenties – the only difference in 1975 was that I was thirty-one years old and had a lot of money.

I had no regular girlfriend during my success years. Prior to this period I'd been in a four-year relationship with Hede, but we had drifted apart after 'Rock 'n' Roll' had been a hit because my schedule kept me away from home so much, and I wasn't keen to start another serious affair. While I was at Mizzards Farm, there were always plenty of girls around the house and I wanted to spread myself about a bit – I was able to get away with so much then as well, so very often I'd have three or more in a bed just because I could. If I wasn't going out but wanted a bit of fun I'd send up one of my assistants in the Rolls-Royce to one of the clubs in town, where they'd tell women I was having a party and invite them back. The girls would usually come out of curiosity – just to see where Gary Glitter lived – but would soon get into the party spirit. Or if I was by myself down there I'd phone up Kathy, a girl I had a casual relationship with who worked at the Playboy Club. I'd ask her to round up some girls and some coke, and rent-a-party would turn up at about 4 a.m. We'd make merry until about ten the next day, after which everybody would sleep through to mid-afternoon and then either continue where they'd left off or head back to town.

Mayfair magazine used the house for photo locations quite a lot, and often the photographer would pack up and leave while the girls stayed behind. Occasionally girls would move in, but they never stayed longer than about a month because I think my lifestyle got a bit too much for them. There wasn't any time to fall in love: it was more a matter of falling into bed, waking up in some strange position and starting again. I was living the life of a playboy and loving every minute of it.

The closest I ever came to a lasting relationship was with Michelle First, who's now married to the heir to the Heron Group. Mikki was seventeen when I met her – she had come down with a crowd that had been rounded up at the Speakeasy – just out of college and beautiful. She stayed with me for about a year, during which time I paid for her to go on a modelling course, and she became very successful. We did find out that we had something very good going but by that time I was going broke and she was on the way up. That was what split us up, because she was mingling with the super-rich and I felt rather intimidated knowing I was in financial trouble. Under different circumstances I think we could have been very happy, and we're still good friends even though I hardly ever see her.

In 1975 I passed my driving test, which was something of a long-standing ambition as I'd had two cars – a Rolls-Royce and a mini – for a year. The Rolls-Royce was the fulfilment of a childhood dream for me: ever since Uncle Stape had taken my cousins and me to the circus in London in what I thought was a Rolls, I had vowed I wasn't going to buy a car until I could afford one of those. In my mind no other car could come close to it: they had such a beautiful antique quality that to me they were like a piece of art. This took place during the 'Buy British' campaign, too, and I felt I had to do just that because I was in the public eye and so much of my earnings came from the UK. When I bought the car I used to practise in it with James, my assistant. I had L plates tied on the bumpers, and every time we parked somewhere they'd get stolen.

I took my test in the Rolls, after my Uncle John, who owned a driving school, had given me an intensive course of lessons. I felt a bit sorry for the examiner, because there was no way he could fail me – we'd turned my test into a media event, and all the Fleet Street photographers were outside the centre waiting for the picture of me tearing up my L plates! The poor man looked rather stunned when I turned up in a Rolls-Royce wearing a fur coat and platform shoes, and he let me get away with a couple of outrageous acts as we went round. I turned the wrong way up a one-way street, and when he pointed it out I told him I was just checking he was paying attention. Later, when he banged his book on the dashboard for the emergency stop, before I hit the brake I held him back in his seat and said: 'Be careful now!' He really didn't know what to make of me – he definitely wasn't in the Gang – but he certainly didn't intend to be all over the papers as the man who had failed Gary Glitter.

I'm not sure he knew what he was letting Hampshire in for when he pased me, because although the Silver Cloud is the best car to be driven in it's not a great car to drive – at least, not at any speed other than sedate. My particular one became lethal in the wet and wouldn't take corners any faster than about five miles per hour. Once, when I had my son and several of his friends in the back, I approached a T-junction too fast and, knowing it would be impossible to turn, opted to hit a tree head on instead. I did £2,000 worth of damage to the car and had to pay for the tree I knocked down. After that I had special tyres fitted to give the car a lot more grip in the rain. The only other accident I've had was actually very funny. I was driving home at about 2 a.m., somewhat the worse for wear, and stopped in the driveway to pet the horse that a little girl from the village grazed in my paddock. It was the kind of misty late autumn night that Dracula would have loved, and when I couldn't see Star at his usual place by the fence I got out and left the engine running. A minute or so later I leaned in to switch it off and knocked the column shift into reverse – as Rolls-Royces are adjusted to pull themselves along, it started off back down the drive with me trotting beside it, caught up in the steering wheel. In the road it reversed into a ditch, turned over and rocked back on to its boot with the front sticking up in the air. I had freed myself by now, but still ended up in the stream absolutely soaked – it sobered me up immediately. The next morning, when the local garage arrived to pull the car out, the guys stared at it for about a quarter of an hour; they were completely baffled as to how I had managed to get it into that position!

The fact that I had only these two accidents was little short of miraculous given that my most travelled route was between my house and the pub. Very often the local copper, Nigel, would pull me over, shove me into the passenger seat, drive me home and put me to bed. I'm still thanking God that I never killed anybody, because sometimes I was behind that wheel in an absolutely terrible state. Remarkably, I didn't get nicked for over a year, and even then I wasn't nearly as drunk as I might have been. It was the day after I'd finished some shows, and although I always got somebody to drive the car for me on tour, as soon as we were finished I'd want to get rid of everybody and so I'd drive myself home. Our last show was in Cardiff, and on my way back I stopped in Dorset for dinner at the pub that Douglas, my personal assistant, had bought. Although he offered to put me up for the night I wanted to get back to my own bed, so I made a point of not drinking anything except one glass of wine. As I left, though, the villagers lined up outside singing, 'Come on! Come on!' and bought me a huge glass of port. Not wanting to offend, I downed it before I drove away and got pulled up by the police about a hundred yards along the road. I was breathalysed, failed the test, and started arguing with the policeman – I told him there was nobody on the road and, anyway, he could easily drive the car back to Douglas's for me where I could have stayed the night. He wasn't impressed. I was taken in and then got very stroppy at the police station – I refused to give a blood sample, as I was sure I still had alcohol in my system from the massive end-of-tour booze-up the night before. I behaved badly because I was too used to getting away with it – the fact that I was Gary Glitter usually ensured that I got special treatment. Looking back, I could have got myself in much more serious trouble as they might have made a point of searching my car where I'd forgotten I had put some dope. As it was, I got fined £100 and banned for a year. The next time I got nicked was in 1981 after I'd been abroad for two years, and although I know it happened in Essex, I was too out of it to remember any details. I got banned for three years that time, and for the fifteen years I've held a licence I've been unable to use it for more than half of that time.

I drank a great deal during 1975 and 1976, but my drug dependency over that period is something that has been continually overstated. The only drug I used to take in any quantity was speed, and that was because of my workload – in the beginning I had no idea I could actually tell anybody I wasn't going to do something because I was exhausted, so I'd say 'Yes' to everything. My years in Germany had left me with a detailed knowledge of what to take to stay awake so that became the easiest way to keep going and meet the seemingly impossible deadlines being set for me. The only problem is that once I started I became reliant on it. It happened very quickly, and I had to start taking other stuff to counterbalance it when I wasn't working. It was the kind of situation that becomes a merry-go-round of taking uppers and downers just so you can do what you ought to be doing naturally.

My perpetual weight problem added to this, too. After the first *Top of the Pops* I was twelve stone, and Mike put me on a diet; but I couldn't really stick to it, so I went to Dr Newton, a private doctor in Harley Street who's been struck off now. He gave me injections of pregnant sheep's urine, prescribed a course of slimming tablets – amphetamines – and put me on a lean red meat-only diet. The pounds dropped off. So I'd go to see him for the two weeks before I had to do *Top of the Pops* – we could plan in advance for it just by looking at my release schedule – but as soon as the treatment finished I'd blow up like a balloon in just a few days. The contrast between that and what I had been was so great I used to think I looked like the Michelin Man, so then I would start taking more slimming pills to bring my weight back down. This wild fluctuating of my weight caused me a great deal of anguish over the years. I was in a considerable amount of pain, too, as performing in and walking about in those towering platform shoes isn't exactly the best thing you can do for your spine. The speed used to relieve this discomfort, and I didn't then realise that regular massage would have the same effect.

I didn't do a great deal of recreational drug-taking, though, so when I was at Mizzards Farm, and not working so hard, I would do my best to get away from dope. Cocaine was there occasionally, but at that time it wasn't readily available in London and was very expensive, so I only dabbled. The few times I tripped on LSD were when somebody slipped it to me. I accidentally snorted some heroin once, thinking it was coke; quite luckily it made me so sick, that after that I wouldn't have the stuff near me. Hash made me paranoid, but I did develop a taste for Thai grass: at Christmas in 1975 I bought eighty foot-long Thai sticks, and after my family had gone some friends and I got through them all while perpetually playing Dr Hook's *Bankrupt* album – it was a hilarious week. I was never a great smoker, though, as I didn't get much enjoyment out of being laid back – Gary Glitter was meant to be an up sort of character.

Drinking used to take the edge off the speed when I wanted to relax, but I won't deny I liked it. I was very fond of strong beers – I used to start the day with two or three bottles just to get me going – but had to cut them out due to the calories. I didn't drink a lot of hard liquor at that time: I liked the taste of gin and tonic, but too much would depress me; whisky didn't interest me at all, unless it was a good single malt which I could only really get in Scotland. If I wanted to pretend I wasn't drinking I'd go on to vodka and tonic and make out it was lemonade, and it wasn't until later that I acquired a taste for brandy and went on tequila benders. Mostly I liked wine, and as I became wealthy and got to know more about it I started to appreciate better quality. I still believe that nothing can compare with the inner glow I got from good wine, and I'd think nothing of opening a £50 bottle, pouring it into a tall glass and drinking the whole lot myself! Champagne was a favourite, too, as it had a very uplifting effect and went very well with the image. The extravagance shown by Gary Glitter shouting for more champagne was precisely what I was trying to get across – the average person's idea of pop star behaviour.

On reflection, it seems as if I had the self-destruct button firmly depressed, but if I did it wasn't at all a conscious thing. It was simply that everything was so available to me and I wanted it all. Just like when I used to hang around Mike's office in 1971, I didn't want to miss out on anything, and once I had got there I felt it was my duty to be as over the top and eccentric as possible. I was following Keith Moon's advice and not treating life as a dress rehearsal, but instead was relishing my hard-earned success. However, in those days I was still really learning the role and didn't know I could do it without a few drinks inside me. Neither did I quite realise when to stop playing King of the Castle and go back to work.

The second half of 1975 in my house was a wonderful period, but all through that year I had been earning far less than in the previous two. I went out on the road fewer times; I wasn't writing with Mike, because while I was having fun in Hampshire he was spending more and more time in the house he'd bought in Majorca; I only released three singles – just one of which, 'Doin' Alright with the Boys', was a substantial hit; and the album I'd made in America had hardly sold at all. My way of thinking was that, after working so hard with so little time off, I was entitled to enjoy my new home for a while. The simple truth, however, was that I'd started to get lazy, and while I was spending more and more money there was very little coming in.

My attitude towards money hadn't really changed since I was a teenager in London – if I had it I'd spend it. As I had grown up with the Elvis Manual of Rock Stardom, I honestly believed that being a pop star was 90 per cent about keeping up appearances. When I was earning £100 per week in the late fifties, nearly all of it would be spent on clothes. It was just as important to me to show off to myself as to other people. When I first left home, if I was in the West End with only a pound to my name, instead of making it last so I could eat for the whole week I'd blow it all on a cup of tea in the Ritz, because that made me feel good. In 1975 and 1976, when I was living the role of Gary Glitter, it was just as important to my own sense of worth that I had the best of everything. I had the public to consider as well: one of the reasons they latched on to Glitter in the first place was the escapism and glamour factor offered by its excess. They expected me to travel first class, to stay in the best hotels, to drink vintage champagne in the best restaurants, to live in a huge house and to do everything they would do if they were me. I felt that by buying my records and coming to see my shows they were investing in Gary Glitter, as opposed to Slade or the Sweet, and the least I could do was give them a return. The cost of my lifestyle was the company overheads.

I took my responsibilities seriously, and being Gary Glitter cost a great deal of money. My Glitter clothes worked out at between £2,000 and £3,000 a suit, because the sequins were imported from Switzerland. I could have had domestic-made ones, but all the other glam stars used those and so Gary Glitter had to go one better. I had about thirty of those suits, and around fifty pairs of shoes and boots at an average of £50 a pair. I needed that number as I wore them all the time at home: there were always people around and it's what they wanted from me – just like anybody today would be disappointed if they dropped in on Prince and found him slopping about in an old cardigan.

All the limousines, hotel room-service bills and receptions that the record company laid on for the press were coming out of *my* royalties, but I was never really aware of it. I didn't stop to think who eventually footed the bills for things like the American promotion trip or the time I flew across the Atlantic three times in as many days. It was naïve of me, but while I was enjoying myself getting pissed and gadding about at what I assumed was somebody else's expense, I never once stopped to consider who that somebody else was.

The big difficulty I had with curbing my spending though – apart from the fact that I didn't really want to – was that I had reached a point at which I never carried cash. Everything was charged to accounts, or

I'd sign bills that would be sent to the office, and consequently I'd spend much more than if I'd been given actual wads of cash that I could see getting smaller. Signing a £5,000 tailor's bill was as easy as signing a £50 restaurant bill, and I never took any notice of the amount on my account at the butcher's or my slate behind the bar at the village pub.

When I was out with other rock stars, it was usually my credit card that ended up on the table at the end of the night – Rod was terrible for that: he never ever put his hand in his pocket. Once I invited Paul and Linda McCartney out for dinner at Morton's, a club on Berkeley Square; they turned up with five other people whom I didn't even know and left me with the bill. I think I used to bring a lot of this on myself, though, because I was still a little overwhelmed by many longer-established stars. Being new to fame, I was always much keener than them to be out and about all the time, and liked the idea of hanging out with the big names: I'd often ring up somebody and ask them to go out to dinner, and if they hesitated I'd say it was on me. I don't think I was confident enough around them to insist they paid their share, either.

I was paying a lot of wages, too, both directly and indirectly. I had my personal entourage, which had swollen to include secretaries, valets, drivers and personal assistants, all of whom seemed to have their own assistants. But, again harking back to Elvis, it was my mafia – a very necessary part of being a star. As well as paying their salaries I was paying their bills; when they came out with me I'd insist on them acting as showbiz as I did because we were in the entertainment industry. We were 'on' all the time, so it was champagne and lobster thermidor all round. Mike had been as affected by the success as I had, and RAM had expanded from half a dozen people in Regent Street to a huge, rather grand suite in Conduit Street with a much bigger staff. The overheads, including the wage bill for assistants and assistants' assistants, was now massive, and my earnings were supporting that as well.

Everybody in the organisation, including me, but with the exception of maybe Ray Brown and Jef Hanlon, thought the success would last for ever – if the last record was a hit, then why shouldn't the next one be a hit as well? It happens to most pop stars: they get three hit records in a row, start receiving some royalty payments after about a year and assume they're set up for life. It's a fatal mistake to make.

I could have learnt a great deal about looking after my own business affairs from Rod. Often, while I was round at his house, he'd tell me to go and have a swim or something while he went into his study for a meeting with his accountants. I knew what he was doing, but I didn't think I needed my own accountants checking over the books at the management office and then reporting back to me on what was coming in and going out. Mike and Ray were taking care of all the business, and I was quite prepared to let them carry on doing so – they were my best mates. I never looked at a bank statement in all those years; I think I was a bit frightened about the concept of business, but I hadn't even paid sufficient attention to realise that it was just a matter of simple arithmetic: too much was going out, with not enough coming in.

I'm not pointing the finger at them at all: the situation was entirely of my own making through my over-spending. Further to that, though, I refused to be told what was going on when people began to get worried that things were getting out of hand. Ray and the others from the office literally couldn't get through to me. I was a couple of hundred miles away from London most of the time, and by mid-1976 had built a wall of people round me who were completely independent from the RAM office – my posse worked for me, and if I told them to tell Ray I was out, they would. The only time I ever contacted the office was if the champagne dispenser in my fridge wasn't working or if I wanted them to sort out a plumber for me. That's how ridiculous it was: I was paying an assistant in Hampshire to ring a secretary in London, whose wages I also paid, to find a plumber in Hampshire who could unblock my sink, and then the girl in London would have to ring the girl in Hampshire to tell her when he was coming!

Ray tried to talk to me about it, but I wouldn't let him. I can remember him taking me out to lunch at the end of 1975, showing me some sheets of figures and telling me the books simply couldn't be balanced because I wasn't earning as much as I was spending. But by then I was so out of it through the booze that I didn't even look at them. I waved them away and said, 'OK, OK, now let's get on with the real business of having a drink and a spot of lunch!' I genuinely didn't care.

9
Farewell

Mike and I were still feeling fairly complacent when we booked a tour for March 1976, but after tickets had been on sale for a month it became clear that this show wasn't going to sell out. The indications were that we would do well enough to make money from it, but for Mike this was far from satisfactory – every Gary Glitter tour *had* to sell out. I was still down in the country not giving things any serious thought, but up in London Mike and Tony Barrow were tearing their hair out and came up with one of the few schemes in whose conception I had no part. They decided this was to be my farewell tour, the last chance the public would ever get to see Gary Glitter on stage. The announcement of my retirement was purely a scam to sell tickets, and I went along with it because I couldn't be bothered to argue.

It was really quite daft to have got so upset about my popularity falling off, because the reasons were obvious: the pop music cycle, that then lasted about five years, had come full circle. If glam rock wasn't quite dead by early 1976, it was definitely on its last legs. Slade and Mud were about the only groups still releasing, and their singles were barely scraping the Top 30. The lifespan of teenie-appeal, essentially singles-selling groups, will always be finite because the fans quite simply grow out of them – the large percentage of my audience had been ten-, eleven- and twelve-year-olds who watched me on *Top of the Pops*, but four years later they were through puberty. Suddenly being cool was all-important, and they couldn't be seen to be still into the same music they'd listened to as children. Then, as their younger brothers and sisters got to an age when they started taking an interest in pop music, they didn't want to inherit other people's idols, so they discovered their own. The groups Our Kid and Slik attempted to fill the gap left by the decline of glam, but they didn't last long because they were too much in the mould of the Sweet or the Bay City Rollers. By 1976 disco was taking over the charts. It's a common misconception that disco music didn't break in Britain until *Saturday Night Fever*, which wasn't until late 1977/ early 1978; it was in fact merely a consolidation of what had been going on for two years already – in 1976 the artists selling singles were the Real Thing, Candi Staton, Tina Charles, Billy Ocean, Barry White and Donna Summer – and happening in the clubs for even longer than that.

Mike and I had been believing our own press for some time by then and had reached the point at which we thought the normal rules didn't apply to Glitter; that's why he took it so badly when the tour wasn't selling out. But in reality we were simply going to the wall one time too many – a remarkable reaction, considering he wasn't completely blind to the writing on the wall. We'd tried to change our approach earlier that year when writing and recording 'You Belong to Me' – I had the Four Tops in mind when I was writing my bits, and Mike put it together with a brilliant Motown-ish, funky beat. I believe, musically, it was the best record we ever made, but when it came out in March it got no higher than Number 30.

We didn't attempt to build on it by following it up in the same vein, which I feel was a big mistake: one I'd made before, too, when in 1975 I took a step in a different direction with 'Love Like You and Me'. Even though Mike got a credit on that song, most of it was written by myself and Gerry Shepherd of the Glitterband; it was the only Gary Glitter/Glitterband studio collaboration ever. I thought it would be an ideal opportunity to attempt the change I knew we were due for, and Gerry and I created a heavy metal sound by working the guitar and bass into a hard-driving free-type riff. It went straight into the Top 10, but that was due to shops over-ordering on the strength of the record before – 'Oh Yes, You're Beautiful', which was a huge hit – and it fell sharply the next week when people weren't actually buying it. I'm still certain we could have got somewhere with that music, and I think it was the too wallowy lyrics of that particular song that put the Glitter fans off: the opening lines were 'Ain't no sunshine just a cloud above my head/life don't come easy'. However, with the next record we opted to play safe and get back with the Gang – Mike and I wrote 'Doin' Alright with the Boys', which was massive. Reverting to type was easy then, but a year later the change in the pop climate had virtually removed it as an option.

After 'You Belong to Me' wasn't a success Mike took the view that nobody would ever want anything different from me, and he wasn't willing to put in the effort to reinvent the character from the ground upwards in the way David Bowie did. He seemed to lose interest, he may have genuinely wanted to call it a day when he thought up the farewell tour scam. I think Ray Brown had had enough at that point too, and although I wouldn't have admitted it then, I realise now that the best thing I could have done was step back from Gary Glitter for a while. So in all honesty, retirement was actually a very good idea, and perhaps that was at the back of my mind when I allowed myself to be talked into it.

What I shouldn't have done, though, was go along with what Mike and Tony had announced to the media as the reason for my retirement. They were told that I was retiring for love – that I was giving everything up to settle down with a girl I'd met. The thinking behind this was that it was about the only thing I hadn't done. Everything we told the press had been a carefully orchestrated campaign to let them see only Gary Glitter the pop star, and the press had always been eager to find out about the man behind the image. Mike told me I had to have a romance now, because for so long there had been an official silence about my private life, and Gary Glitter needed to let the fans know he had one. I said that was because Gary Glitter never had time to get romantically involved; also I argued that I had a very interesting real private life which would probably make much better reading. From my point of view, falling in love and going to live in suburbia would only dent my Jack-the-lad image and remove the hint of availability that makes a difference to fans if they're going to fancy a star seriously.

Mike was adamant, though. He knew it would make front-page news and I'm also convinced that, on a much less Machiavellian level, the idea of me in a relationship appealed to him so much because he'd just got married. We were still best friends, and it must have been awkward for him in his new situation to have me living the life of a playboy, so I'm pretty sure he was trying to push me into settling down. The irony was that a serious and loving relationship was just what I needed at that time – I was feeling very emotionally battered and wished I could have given everything up for love.

I brought up the fact that there was nobody I wanted to retire for, but he wasn't at all worried as he sorted out that trifling detail – Mary Medley, the girl who did his and the Glitterband's hair and whom I'd met once or twice, was willing to go along with it. Eventually Mike sold the idea to me. First of all the story was leaked and Mary and I were seen around town holding hands, then we were pictured holding a ring, and when we threw a huge engagement party the media had a field day. 'Glitter Retires for Love' was splashed over every paper – even the serious ones carried a story – it was a headline on *News at Ten*, and I went on Russell Harty's chat show to tell the full story behind my romance. I was becoming less and less happy, as I had no idea it was going to be so big – nobody did – but by then I was stuck with it. If I'd told the truth at that time a lot of people – whom I saw as my friends – would have been left with egg on their faces. So I played along; I've watched my performance on Russell Harty's show several times since, and it deserves an Oscar!

Naturally, the tour sold out immediately it was

reannounced as the Farewell Tour. Officially, the concert at the New Victoria Theatre in London was to be the last time I ever set foot on stage and it was a very emotional affair – because I'd become the biggest of the glam acts it was perceived as glam's swansong, genuinely the end of an era. Mike Mansfield, director of the hot TV pop show *Supersonic*, came down to film the event, and as many fans were outside the theatre as had tickets to get in. It was the best possible way for me to go out, too, as I might not have been right at the top at that time but the reaction made me feel as if I was. The fans were really upset that something that had been such a part of their lives for nearly four years was now all over, and I could see girls squashed at the front so distraught they were crying their eyes out. I was so affected by the strength of feeling for me in that room that I found it impossible to get through numbers like 'Remember Me This Way' and 'I Love You Love Me Love' without breaking down. When I came off, after taking more bows than I can remember, I was bawling like a baby and felt quite distressed at the fact that the whole event had just been a showbiz trick to sell a few tickets.

After the show Mary and I went on holiday and were photographed at the airport. The story issued was that we were going to travel round the world looking for our own paradise, but I'm certain that by then the newspapers were wise to what was going on. Nobody likes being made a fool of – especially a reporter – and they didn't forgive me until a couple of years ago; even now I'm sure there are a few still bearing a grudge. It upset my fans a great deal, too – they'd been duped. They'd supported me for years, and now I'd let them down by pulling some shabby con. I don't feel unfairly treated by this reaction, though, because it was more my fault than anybody else's – I should have put my foot down when I had the chance.

Mary and I travelled to Portugal; far from being the get-away-from-everybody honeymoon-style holiday we were pretending it was, I'd taken a crowd with me. As well as Ray Brown and his girlfriend and a few others from my entourage, I even had another girl – Inge – with me. We stayed on the Algarve, where Ray played golf, I played around with Inge and Mary sunbathed. Then after two weeks Mary and I said goodbye: she went home, and I went to Thailand with Inge for a month. There was never any hint of a relationship between Mary and me: we did go to bed once, just to see if there was anything there, but we couldn't take it seriously. We parted friends, though – I think she was as embarrassed about the situation as I was. I bumped into her on holiday in Bali recently and she told me she had never held a grudge, even though she suffered some unwanted press attention during the aftermath.

When I got back, Inge came down to stay with me at Mizzards Farm for a while. There was a wonderfully hot summer in 1976, and I took up life with a vengeance – the cricket, the barbecues, the parties. Workwise, however, because I was supposed to have retired I did nothing – I didn't release another record that year – and started enjoying it like that. The whole affair with Mary and the retirement had made me realise that Gary Glitter should go on the back burner for a while. The public had let us know it was time for a rest, and Paul Gadd needed a bit of attention.

Then Ray called me up to London for a meeting to explain to me what terrible financial trouble I was in. Whereas during 1975 I had earned a bit from three singles and an album, this year practically nothing had come in except a few back-catalogue song-writing royalties; yet I was coming to the end of two years of spending as if my income amounted to millions. It seemed that I'd only ever had enough money to do that for twelve months, but because I'd chosen not to listen when I was being told that it wouldn't last for ever, I had assumed it would. As far as I was concerned, for three years there had always been enough money for anything I wanted and certainly as much as I needed to hang out with the likes of Rod and Elton, so I never properly understood the scale of my success as compared to theirs: I had been rich, but I certainly hadn't been *that* rich. My big-earning period was relatively short compared with that of an artist like Rod, and for the first three records – the first of which was my biggest seller – I was only on 3 per cent. What really made the difference between me and the mega-earners, though, was my record sales as part of the global market. I had earned everything possible from the UK and Australia, and had done very well in Europe for two of those four years, but that was all. Britain is only 10 per cent of the world record sales market, Australia has such a small population it's only 2 per cent, and Europeans don't buy many records – so in total it only represents about 8 per cent. Unlike Rod I had no income from the USA, which accounts for over half of the world's record sales, or from Japan or South America, so even at my peak I was only earning 20 per cent of what some of my peers were bringing in.

My big earning years were the Wilson government years, too, when income tax for big earners stood at 87 pence in the pound. I was one of the few in that bracket who had stayed in England – the Stones left, Michael Caine left, Rod left; there was a joke at the time that went: 'Would the last person to leave the UK please turn out the light.' I think I was that last person. I'd been warned about problems with the Inland Revenue over a year previously when I spent a weekend at Rod's house: he came out of a meeting with his accountants and said, quite simply, 'That's it, I've got to go.' I thought he meant go down the pub, but he explained to me why it was impossible for stars to stay in Britain with the current taxation rates. Within a week he'd moved to Los Angeles. He tried to get me to go with him, but I refused because I had no career in America; everything I'd worked for was in Britain and I had family here – although I seldom saw them, I would have missed them if I'd moved to the States. At the meeting in the late summer of 1976, Ray told me that I was going to get serious trouble from the tax man soon, because I still owed on my successful years and there was no money left in the kitty. Also, he said there was a tax inspector called Griffiths who was out to get me as, after the exodus of a couple of years before, the Inland Revenue were determined to make an example out of somebody. He warned me that I would lose my house. But typically, full of booze and bravado, I simply laughed and told Ray that a house was just another responsibility that I didn't really have time for.

It seemed to me there was nothing I could do, so I did exactly that – nothing, until it was too late. I had started to believe I couldn't even work my way out of trouble, because the music scene had changed again as punk began to make headway – although this was the year before the Queen's Silver Jubilee, it was in 1976 that the Sex Pistols put out 'Anarchy in the UK'. The success of that group put the whole Gary Glitter concept in a different light: suddenly it was very unfashionable for rock stars to live it up ostentatiously in country mansions. I had become a dinosaur, and the only offers of work I was getting were the celebrity game show circuit and cabaret clubs. There was a good living to be made in both these areas – in late 1976 the Fiesta in Sheffield, a huge chicken-in-the-basket place, offered me £25,000 to do a week there, which was an absolute fortune then – but I turned them all down. Regardless of the fact that I was losing money hand over fist, I was determined not to end up like Gerry and the Pacemakers.

In December I did manage to get it together to attempt what was called a comeback when I appeared on a TV special, *The Supersonic Royal Christmas Party*. I didn't have the Glitterband with me on the TV show and had to perform a medley of my hits backed by an orchestra, which didn't really please me as it was a bit too cabaret for my taste, but I was in no position to complain. Two things happened, however, that considerably boosted my self-esteem. Marc Bolan was on the bill too, and when a row broke out between Mike and his management over who should headline, Marc himself asked me to do it as he said I was an impossible act to follow. I was immensely grateful, because after a year away I really needed that show of support. After the show all the artists were presented to Princess Margaret, who had been guest of honour. As she was wearing a tiara I commented on how glad I was that she'd worn some glitter. She looked me straight in the eye and said, 'Oh yes, I'll always have some glitter tucked away in my wardrobe.' That really cheered me up: I might have gone broke, but I could still mingle with the aristocracy.

I got a very good reaction from the crowd during that show, and when I put out a single, 'It Takes All Night Long', in February of the following year it went to Number 25. On the strength of it we were sufficiently inspired to go on a tour in March. It was my last chance to get clear of financial ruin, but unfortunately it was a disaster. Jef was no longer handling the booking and promotion for RAM: he'd left after the decision to turn down the club in Sheffield, which was taken against his judgement. So we went to an outside promoter who went broke halfway through the dates. We lost a great deal of our money – money that we didn't have – and that was what finished me off.

The bank foreclosed on my house; Ray informed me I couldn't wait for the right buyer at the right price, but had to take the first offer. That was very upsetting, not only because the place meant a lot to me as the first property I'd ever owned, but because I was set to lose a great deal of money on it – I'd bought in a boom, and when I came to sell the market had hit rock bottom. All the extras I'd put in became worthless. The people who came to look round would say, 'So what if the bath's made of imported Italian marble? I only want a bathroom.' If I'd hung on for another year – and had I known what I know now, I could have done – I could have sold it to an Arab who would have paid a million for all those luxury touches.

Since then, I've never put anything in a house that I can't take with me.

While selling the house had got the bank off my back, the Inland Revenue were closing in like sharks smelling blood. I'd told Rod, back in 1975, that I wasn't going to leave and, rightly or wrongly, I'd hung on for two years; but by that time it had become a case of *having* to go. We booked a short tour of the Republic of Ireland, and broke a rule I'd made four years before that I'd never play another club. We were offered a small fortune to play the opening night of a huge night club in Dublin, and they were going to pay us in cash. I did the date, put £20,000 in a holdall and flew from there to Paris. I didn't set foot in the UK again for over two years.

10
Running Away

When I arrived in Paris I checked into a hotel, with
no idea what I was going to do. I knew I had enough
money to live on for about a year, and as I couldn't
go back to the UK I was under no pressure to meet
any music business commitments. I knew that Hede,
the German girl I'd lived with for four years, was
living there, and she helped me find a lovely five-
roomed apartment in a turning off the Champs
Elysées. We were good friends, but there was never
going to be a rekindling of the affair. She had her own
life in Paris, so I saw her about once a week for dinner
and just settled back to enjoy the city. Apart from
Hede, and a few people from French record companies whom I'd met when I went there to work, I
knew nobody in Paris. I travelled there completely
alone, and I felt much the same as I had felt arriving
in Hamburg over ten years before: everything was
fresh and new, and I was on the verge of an
adventure. And, of course, Paris was a far more
attractive proposition because I wasn't skint.

I couldn't ever remember feeling as relaxed as I felt
at that point. Paris was the perfect place for me to

start bringing my life down to earth because I could do it in stages. If I found I was missing the attention and wanted to prove that Gary Glitter still existed, all I had to do was walk up and down the Champs Elysées and before long I'd bump into some British or Australian tourists who recognised me. Or, if I called attention to myself, French kids too would realise who I was – I'd had one big hit and several lesser ones in France, and used to be on television there a lot. Yet I could also disappear in Paris with equal ease, just by walking round the back streets and keeping myself to myself. That was wonderful. I walked everywhere in Paris, stopping in cafés and poking round in funny little shops, and as I've always been fasinated by architecture I had so much to look at. It was the first time I'd been able to do anything like that in four years, and wandering round Paris took me back to my first visits to London when I was very young and would spend ages just staring up at the buildings. I used to try and imagine how great it would be to have been eighteen and wealthy and packed off to college in Paris for a couple of years.

I started checking out night clubs, too. First of all I'd go to the music business-type hangouts I could remember from when I'd come to the city to do TV or to play live, but they were much the same as music business hangouts in London and not what I was looking for. Then after a few months I bumped into a bunch of kids, all in their late teens, who were real Glitter fans – they'd got all the records and had seen several shows but were just becoming punks and they kind of adopted me, calling me their Godfather. They lived on the outskirts of Paris and would come in to go to the clubs and then stay at my flat. It was convenient for them, because the guys in the group were gay and two of them were very much in love but couldn't stay together in their parents' houses. They looked after me – one of the girls moved in with me – until I left in early 1978.

Those kids knew the Parisian club scene inside out and took me to some really exciting places – one of them, The Palace, was the first place I'd ever seen a laser lightshow in a discotheque. What was really uplifting about these clubs was they weren't exclusive establishments like Tramp, where celebrities go just to be there, but street-level places for real, discriminating music fans who were creating trends in music and dance. They were like the places Mike and I used to get our inspiration from in 1971, and getting into some new music in an environment like that sparked my interest in a way I hadn't felt for a long time. Remarkably though, in spite of the fact that exposure to this scene got my ideas flowing, I didn't want to do anything there. I was offered singing jobs and opportunities to go into the studio, but I think I was enjoying life far too much to want to get back on the treadmill. Perhaps most importantly, though, it taught me how to enjoy music again instead of looking at it as work, as I had come to do in England.

I did get homesick, though. When I first arrived there I missed England terribly, and I felt very sad that I'd had to leave in the way I did – I was so naïve that I honestly didn't understand how I could have had so many hit records, done so many shows, given so much and suddenly become *persona non grata*. In what I think was a defence mechanism against loneliness I thought of my being in Paris as very temporary, a long weekend, and convinced myself that soon I'd be called home. I'd firmly fixed in my mind this idea that I'd just been sent away for a couple of months while the people back in London whom I thought were still working on my behalf sorted out the tax man, arranged a record deal for me and got me my house back – a bit like Oscar Wilde, sent away to Paris while the scandal was hushed up. For quite a while after I arrived I didn't form any strong friendships, which is very unusual for me, because I wanted to keep myself available to go home at short notice.

Of course nothing like this was ever on the cards, and while I was waiting I got lost in Paris, which is very easy to do. It was just as well that I did, as that year was a very important time for me mentally. The whole experience had the effect of making me realise how jaded I'd become – I must have been both very bored and very boring during my last couple of years in England. Understandably, I cut down my drinking a great deal in Paris, because I suddenly had so much to take an interest in. I got my head together to the point that I was Paul Gadd again, and completely understood where Gary Glitter stood in relation to him.

Nearly a year after I'd arrived I was sent a script for *The Rocky Horror Show*, to read with a view to playing Frank-N-Furter in a production in New Zealand. I wasn't particularly interested, even though I'd seen the play when it opened in Chelsea and thought it was good. I was also by then running out of money and knew I would have to do some work – I'd been living very well and spent all of the £20,000 I'd arrived with, plus most of another £10,000 I'd gone and collected from a bank account I had in Jersey. Really, I wasn't over-keen to get into something that might be a bit flakey, especially if it was going to be as far away as New Zealand – the script had arrived via the office in London and nobody there seemed to know much about the production. So I kept the script for about two months without reading it, until Ray Brown phoned up and said I had to make a decision. Then I opened it up and read the opening lines, spoken by my character: 'Unlock a mind, a mind unlock. It's the same as the beginning of the end, do you follow.' It threw me completely, because I wasn't an actor and didn't realise I could just read things off the page, and I started worrying about how on earth I would interpret something like that! Then Ray rang again on Friday and gave me the weekend to make up my mind.

That Saturday I noticed that *The Rocky Horror Picture Show* was playing at a cinema in the Champs Elysées at midnight, and I went down there armed with my script to follow the dialogue. When I got there I found a crowd of punks and freaks waiting to go in – I'd never seen anything like this, because I'd been away while it all went on in England – and began to get interested. It was what went on inside that decided me, though, as I watched the audience shouting out the words of the different characters they were identifying with – I thought this whole participation thing was so rock 'n' roll that I had to do it. I rang Ray on the Monday, and by the end of the week I was on a plane to New Zealand.

The Rocky Horror Show was to tour New Zealand's large cities for three months, and represented an attractive financial proposition. Ray had negotiated for me to get paid a percentage of the ticket sales, which could add up to a great deal as I'd been as big in New Zealand as I had in Australia. However, the arrangements didn't work out as planned. It had been calculated that by selling out the stalls in each theatre the show would turn a profit, so the inducement to get me there was that I was to receive the money from sales of the seats in the circles, which could have worked out at between £500 and £1,000 per show. But two weeks into rehearsals, when they came to start erecting the set at the first theatre, it was discovered that the set had been built without taking the circles into account and the eyeline was all wrong – it was impossible to see large parts of the action from up there and so the theatres' circles became unsaleable. As soon as this was discovered, the director and producers told me they wouldn't blame me if I pulled out and wouldn't hold me to the contract. But they also appealed to me by saying that if I did leave the show couldn't go on and the cast and technicians, who had all put so much into it so far, would be out of work. The cast came and begged me to stay, and as I was already well into the part they won me round. So I did the tour for virtually no money at all – about £500 per week – and I still don't know if that whole business with the set was just a con. I don't think it was, but you never know.

The director did wonders turning me into what passed for an actor, but I had never worked so hard before in my life. My part, a transvestite count, really only meant camping it up, so that wasn't too hard – I stole Tim Curry's voice, and talked like it off set too. But I had real trouble on the technical side: I had great difficulty remembering the lines, and learning to be in the right place on stage at the right time was a problem. To make matters worse, at first costume fitting I fell off the stilettoes and twisted my ankle really badly, so that right up to the opening night of a huge night club in Dublin, and they were going to pay us in cash. I did the date, put £20,000 in a holdall and flew from there to Paris. I didn't set foot in the UK twisted my ankle really badly, so that right up to the opening night I had to do rehearsals in the wheelchair that the Dr Scott character uses! Added to which, although it was a terrific role to play, it was a character that I couldn't relate to at all. I certainly was in tune with the whole spirit of Rocky Horror though – the message is don't dream it, be it, and that to me wasn't too far removed from the true spirit of Glitter.

Despite everything, I thoroughly enjoyed the tour. It caused a few raised eyebrows, as New Zealand is quite a staid country, but it played to sixty thousand people, which out of a total population of only three million was phenomenal. I got very good notices, too. But what pleased me most was becoming part of the team: as a member of a cast doing a play, you get very involved with each other on stage and the audience is almost incidental – it was the same in *A Slice of Saturday Night*. This meant a great deal to me, as in the beginning the cast didn't much like the idea of me coming in: they were all professional actors, and I was just a pop star who had landed the best role. When they found out I wasn't going to lord it over them, however, we got on very well. I taught them a rock 'n' roll lifestyle, too – silly stuff, like when, at the hotel in Christchurch, I dared them to streak from the hotel through a fountain in the square opposite and back again. A lot of the young actors took to whooping it up so readily that there were quite a few divorces and broken relationships as a result.

The problem I had, though, was that I started taking a lot of amphetamines while I was working – truck drivers' specials, they were called down there. I hadn't taken anything at all in Paris, but as soon as I stepped back on to a stage I found I had to have something to give me that rush and lift my performance. I got told off by the director a couple of times because of it: in the play I have to go to bed with Janet, one of the very straight couple who get caught up in the weirdness, and got quite aggressively carried away with the scene as a result of taking these pills.

That was one of the problems; the others were considerably more serious. First of all, quite soon after I arrived I got a letter from American Express telling me not to use my card again but to cut it up and send it back, so I knew nobody was paying the bills back at home. Then a few weeks later I had a phone call from London informing me that RAM had ceased trading, so the company that I was hoping was going to sort out my mess at home didn't exist any more. It also left me several thousand miles from home with no cash – the couple of grand I'd brought with me from Paris was long gone – and no management. What really hurt, though, was to be told this by phone, and not even by Ray or Mike but one of the office staff. I thought that after all we had been through Mike especially owed me that at least. Finally, when the tour was nearly over I had a letter telling me that bankruptcy proceedings were being started against me. It was American Express that was taking me to court; the Inland Revenue never do so because it doesn't help them get their money quickly, but as somebody else had started proceedings the tax man had become a creditor.

The show was about to finish and suddenly I felt extremely alone. I started drinking more, and built up my intake fairly quickly. I didn't consciously say I was going on a bender, but that's what happened – I started getting very drunk more and more often until the binges started running into each other and it became a bender. I felt very let down, I wasn't attaching any blame, because I knew I was my own man and ultimately responsible for my own situations. However, although I was also very aware that I'd been through a stage when I was impossible to talk to, I did think people around me hadn't perhaps done everything they could. A few people had made a very good living out of me over the previous four years; surely they owed me enough to keep an eye on me and get me through problem patches? Because I was so far away, though, I had no way of finding out if everybody had done everything they could right up to the end. I was very hurt on a wider scale than that, too. The strange part about being an entertainer or a singer is that you feel you're constantly giving – once you become successful, the degree to which you become public property increases proportionately. At that point, after giving so much, it seemed very unfair that I was to be stripped of everything I had left.

I felt very negative about everything, and my attitude was that I might as well enjoy what I had because I wasn't going to have anything at all for much longer. I had made no money at all out of *Rocky Horror*, but I had a round-the-world-ticket and, for the time being, an American Express card, so I figured: why go back straightaway? All I had waiting for me was a court case. So I decided to take my time and stop off in Tahiti for a holiday; I needed a rest after the very straining tour, and after spending three months wearing stockings and suspenders every night I needed to get my head together for more reasons than my financial situation. My state of mind was therefore fairly fragile when I got a phone call from David Ginges, the Australian promoter who had handled my first tour there, who invited me to come to visit him in Sydney. At first I refused, because I'd been huge in Australia and was embarrassed to go there under the present circumstances. But when I told David about the bankruptcy he talked me into going, telling me not to worry about money as this was the least he could do for me after what I'd done for the business. That attitude really cheered me up and I agreed to go, on the condition he let me use my American Express card for everything I could – this was in the days before computerised systems, and I knew I'd be able to get away with using it for quite a while. I still don't know if David had received a call from Ray asking him to look after me, because I was in a state in which I might have done something silly. It wouldn't have surprised me, even though he told me he saw a newspaper advertisement for the play and tracked me down. So it might just have been fate.

I just relaxed at his house in Sydney for a few days and then he asked me if I wanted to see something of the country, as I'd been to Australia dozens of times but had only ever seen dressing rooms, hotel suites, TV studios and airport lounges. I told him what I really wanted to do was get in a car and drive a thousand miles; wherever I ended up was where I wanted to stay. Australia was big enough to do that, and it appealed to my sense of adventure. He was very keen, so he drew a wad of cash out of the bank, I hired a car on my card and we set off up the Pacific Highway – a lads-together holiday, just hanging out, getting stoned and seeing what came our way.

We drove north round the NSW coast up to Coff's Harbour, where we stayed overnight with one of David's cousins. As we got into Queensland, past Surfer's Paradise and Sunshine Beach, the climate started to change and we were driving past the type of lush vegetation that's found in the tropics. I began to tingle with excitement – I knew we were heading somewhere special. We stopped after almost exactly a thousand miles at a place called Noosa Heads, and I immediately felt as if this was the place I'd been looking for after nearly eighteen months of roaming the globe.

The place is a luxury resort now, but at that time people had only just started to discover it and it was still unspoilt – not much more than a village with a main street and the houses very spread out; it was set in beautiful surroundings with streams, waterfalls, wooded areas and a fabulous beach. Noosa was very bohemian, much like a hippy colony, and most of the people there were professionals who had dropped out of the rat race and moved down from Brisbane, which was not far to the north. There were a lot of weekend hippies too, who would come down from Friday night to Monday morning for a bit of free love and good grass. The minute I stepped out of the car I was recognised, but it was very cool – passers-by would look at me and say something like, 'G'day mate. 'Ere, aren't you Gary Glitter?' then shake hands and be on their way. I felt instantly accepted, so we went straight to an estate agent and fixed up a house to rent. Even from the photos we saw it looked a beautiful place, but when we got there we discovered it overlooked a nudist beach! I thought I'd died and gone to heaven. I knew I'd have to go back to London and face the music at some stage, but I was going to put it off as long as possible; for the time being this was the ideal place to disappear to. We'd rented the house for a month and didn't really expect to stay that long, but as it turned out I remained in Noosa for the best part of the year.

The reason I was able to stay as long as I did with no money at all was due to a complete chance – and rather chancey – meeting in a local restaurant after I'd been there a couple of weeks. David and I had gone into town to eat and noticed, parked outside the café, the biggest limousine I'd ever seen. Inside the place was a group of about eight very tough-looking guys who were obviously with the car. Both they and the car seemed completely out of place in a town as laid back as Noosa, but we took no notice and got on with our meal. Then, suddenly, the guy who seemed to be their head man in the posse shouted over, in the broadest of Sydney accents, 'Oi, Glitter! Come over here!' In spite of a tone I wasn't going to argue with, I decided to ignore it. Then he yelled again, 'Oi, Glitter! Didn't you hear me? Now move yourself!' This time I went over, and by then I was actually rather scared. He looked at me for a few seconds with a really piercing stare, and when he opened his mouth I was sure it was to give the order to have me killed. But all he said was, 'We're up here for the weekend, and I want you to come to my party.' I agreed, but it must have been obvious I had no intention of going anywhere near his party because he added, 'Don't give me any of your crap – I mean it. You've got to come. I'm giving it in your honour.' I felt as if I'd just been made an offer I couldn't refuse.

His name was Richard – that's the only name anybody used, as it turned out he was permanently on the run. He was a drug runner – a very serious gangster who was capable of just about anything – but to me he was the perfect gentleman. Not the sort of character I would usually go out of my way to associate with, but back then he just came across as a very lovely guy. I haven't kept in touch with him, although we've got some mutual friends and so I know he is unable to return to Australia and lives in Amsterdam now.

His party was a very odd affair, as everybody was on magic mushrooms. They were very prevalent in Noosa and, as they tasted absolutely horrible, people would cook them into a sweet soup with a lot of honey. I'd never been exposed to them before, and as I got stuck into this soup 'hallucinations' isn't a strong enough word for what happened to me! It seemed to me that the room and everything and everybody in it was jumping, and I couldn't stop laughing. Everything was funny – not just to me either: everybody was laughing for twenty-four hours. At the end of the party a typhoon passed by. It was out at sea, but still generated winds strong enough to bend the trees double and move cars about. I was terrified, but at the same time I couldn't stop laughing at what was going on outside the window!

When all this had worn off Richard asked me what I was doing in Australia, and I told him about being broke. He couldn't believe it: like so many people who had only seen what I'd wanted them to see, he assumed I'd earned millions. When I convinced him, though, he told me he was going back to Sydney the next day, but his house was mine to live in for as long as I wanted, and he left me a big bundle of cash and access to his charge accounts. He said he was doing this because from 1972 to 1976 he'd served four years in Brixton prison, where the most important part of the inmates' week was watching me on *Top of the Pops*. He said it was the laugh they got from that that kept many of them going through their sentences – and this was his way of repaying me. I didn't feel bad about taking it, either; in a strange way I look on it as a loan, because it wouldn't surprise me if he turned up on my doorstep one day and needed me to do the same for him. Which I would.

It was just what I needed, too. I wasn't ready to go back yet, but David's wife had let him know it would be a good idea for him to go home soon. Now I could stay on in a place that was like paradise on earth while I sorted things out in my mind, and I could live very well – it wasn't necessary to have a lot of money in Noosa, but having a lovely house with a pool made a lot of difference. Throughout my life I've been incredibly lucky in one respect – people have always been there with exactly what I needed at exactly the right time.

Noosa in 1978–9 had an absolutely fabulous ambience. I used to go walking on the beach and lie in the sun there most afternoons – nobody swam in the sea because there were a lot of very poisonous jellyfish just offshore. As an example of how laid back the situation was, I'd see the same girl on the beach with her dog every day; I'd say hello and about a quarter of an hour later she'd answer; then we'd sit there looking at each other for about half an hour. It was like life in slow motion.

There weren't many people there, and we'd continually drop into each other's houses where we had one party after another – no sleep until bedtime, and not much after that! I didn't fall in love specifically – I fell in love with everybody and the place. At night there would always be about twenty people in somebody's house, and everybody ended up in bed together. I lived like a luxurious hippy: I grew my hair halfway down my back, the most I ever wore was shorts and sandals, and I was very stoned most of the time. That was surprising, as I've never been a smoker, but they grew excellent grass in Noosa and it fitted in so well with the way of life. I practically gave up drinking, too – all I'd ever drink was the occasional beer during the day, which would be sweated out virtually as soon as I'd downed it, or a glass or two of wine with meals. It just wasn't necessary to get drunk.

The reason I left Noosa was quite simple – it came to a point when I either had to leave or stay for ever. I had some very attractive offers: I could have gone into real estate because the place was just starting to boom, I could have run clubs or restaurants or just been a kept man – I'm always good value at dinner parties. I wasn't yet ready to drop out completely, though, and in the summer of 1979 I felt it was time to move on. I'd come to terms with the hurt and confusion I'd been feeling a year before and knew it would be best to go back and try to sort things out properly. I was a bit homesick, too – I'd been away for two years and was definitely missing my family, my children, my friends, my music and my fans – everything that had made me what I was.

And I got bored. After chilling out so completely I

got bored to tears and found myself singing and playing the guitar in bars and restaurants. It was the nearest I'd come to Gary Glitter since the tour in Ireland back in 1977, and it was fun. It reminded me of what I'd always done, and made me rediscover how much I liked it. As soon as I made my mind up that I was going home I went back down to David's house in Sydney and got on the phone to see if I could track down anybody who could fix me up some dates.

11
Coming Back

The optimism and expectancy I'd felt when I left Noosa didn't last long in Sydney. I couldn't reach Ray or Mike and the only offer open to me was in the form of a telex sent a couple of weeks previously by Mike Mingard; he had been one of my tour managers from the Glitter days and by now had set up a management company with Angie and Ruth McCartney, Paul's stepmother and stepsister in Birkenhead. Mike said he would be able to put together a tour of cabaret venues and larger clubs for me: places like Baileys in Watford, the Golden Garter in Manchester and the Hummingbird in Birmingham. They were the venues I'd vowed I'd never do, but after talking it over with David I decided that if I was serious about reactivating my career I would have to start somewhere. I figured that at least I wouldn't be going home to absolutely nothing, so I rang Mike Mingard and agreed to do the dates.

Getting back to do them, however, was another matter. I thought I was ready to leave, I was booked on a flight and Mike Mingard was going to meet me at Heathrow, as were my ex-wife Ann and my kids

Paul and Sarah – Ann had been in contact with David while I was in Noosa, and was very worried about me. But I couldn't go. I got as far as the airport with David and his wife, but there I lost my nerve completely and just couldn't go through to the departure lounge. That had never happened to me before – I was renowned for being able to front out any situation. It was actually quite a frightening experience because it left me thinking that if my bottle had really gone then I'd never be able to get back on a stage and perform.

I went back to David's house and started making phone calls to try and explain what had happened, but that was difficult because I wasn't really sure myself. The incident didn't go down well at all with Mike Mingard, who had not only laid out a great deal of money on advertising and promoting the tour, but had to pay cancellation fees to several of the venues. I couldn't think of anything to do. I didn't want to go back to Noosa because I felt I'd made my break with the place, so I stayed with David, basically just feeling sorry for myself and complaining, completely unjustifiably, about the situation I was in – I must have seriously got on David and his wife's nerves, but if I did they didn't let on.

After about a month Mike Mingard rang up and said he had managed to salvage some of the bookings he had made, and put together a few more. He also said I had to go back and do these dates whether I wanted to or not: it was the only hope he had of recovering the money he'd lost on the cancelled tour, and if I didn't show a second time it would be doubtful I'd ever get a third chance anywhere in the UK. That shook me up quite a bit, enough to make me stop thinking about myself and realise I had responsibilities to other people. All Mike had tried to do was help me, so the least I could do was stop being silly. That time I got on the flight.

I had nowhere to stay when I got back and no money at all, so Ann put me up at her house in Clapham. It was convenient because it was in London, and I enjoyed having my children around me, but during the month before the tour started I began to get very depressed. Now, however, I don't believe depression is a strong enough word for what I was feeling. After I'd been there for about two weeks Ann had a barbecue to which she invited my mother and other members of the family, and a few of our mutural friends. I was drinking quite heavily and I know my Mum had just said something to me – but I can't remember what – when I went upstairs to the room I was using. I had some sleeping tablets there, Mandrax, and I started to take them one after another. I don't know what happened next, but I've been told that Ann had wondered where I'd gone and got worried, then found me upstairs unconscious and called an ambulance when she saw the empty pill bottle. I woke up in Wandsworth Hospital after I'd had my stomach pumped out.

Looking back at it, I can honestly say that I had no premeditated plan to kill myself. I don't believe anybody who attempts suicide does think about it logically first – I think that a person gets into a state in which they feel so absolutely low that they genuinely don't know what they're doing. I know I was in a terrible state at that time – utterly distraught emotionally. I'd just spent ten months in luxury in a tropical paradise and was now living in a spare room in south London – and I'd ducked out of returning once, so that shows how keen I was. I was getting ready for a tour I couldn't begin to get excited about, and, really to rub my nose in it, I was going to do it for practically nothing in the same type of venues that I had turned down in 1976 when they were offering a fortune. I was so broke I couldn't afford a cab fare, but because just four years previously I had been one of the biggest stars in the country, I couldn't let myself be seen getting on a bus and therefore had to impose on others for lifts. I had brankruptcy proceedings looming, with a court date set for six months' time. But I think what really triggered it off at Ann's barbecue was that everybody who genuinely loved me was there, and as I looked round at them I felt as if I'd let everybody down, especially young Paul and Sarah.

However, despite the amount I'd had to drink, I can remember actually taking the pills as if I was somebody else watching me – somebody else who was far too fascinated to try to stop what was going on. I tipped them out on to the table by the bed and began to swallow them one by one, washing them down with whatever drink I'd brought in from the garden. Tears were literally pouring down my face, but the strange thing was that I wasn't actually crying – it was completely silent, streaming like a waterfall rather than individual tears. It was as if all the misery and hurt I'd ever felt in my entire life had bottled those tears up inside, but at this point they were overflowing and there was absolutely nothing I could do to stop them. It still makes me go cold when I think about it today. I discharged myself from the hospital before the psychiatrist could get his hands on me. I was very shaken by the whole incident, and vowed to hurl myself back into work to try and make amends for all the anguish I'd caused people.

The only good thing about that tour was the band: it was a six-piece outfit that Mike Mingard had put together, and they were older musicians who had all been around in the rock 'n' roll days and knew how to kick it; we could only afford one drummer, but he was Tony Leonard from the Glitterband who was so good he made up for it. Other than the enjoyment of working with them, as soon as the excitement of being back on stage as Gary Glitter for the first time in over two years wore off, the tour was as awful as I thought it would be. The audiences were as interested in their meals as they were in the music, and it simply wasn't rock 'n' roll – we weren't allowed to get the guitars too loud, we couldn't afford any props or effects, and the stages were all too small for me to get really stuck into my act. I hit the hard liquor in a way I'd never done before during those dates – vodka, brandy, tequila, practically anything – and started taking more and more amphetamines to get up enough to do it with any enthusiasm. I'd only been back for about three months and I was already on the merry-go-round.

I went to court for my bankruptcy hearing on 24 April 1980. Mike Mingard was now my manager and had taken legal advice. He instructed me on how to behave in front of the judge – apologetic almost to the point of being humble, and eager to pay everything back as quickly as possible. However, probably because I was so out of it most of the time I found it very difficult to take seriously. On the day I was anything but modest. I acted as if I was on stage giving a performance: the judge was incredibly dry, and as the court began to take account of my outgoings he peered over his spectacles at me and asked, 'What? £6,000 for bedroom curtains?' I replied, rather chirpily, 'Oh yes, your honour, they were handstitched silk with electric motors and light-sensitive switches!' It didn't go down well at all.

His only other comment was to state how baffled he was that anybody could spend £25,000 on a bathroom, so I answered by describing the quarry in Italy where the marble had come from and asked him if he knew it. He gave me a look which would have got me thrown in the cells if it was possible.

The outcome was never in doubt – I had more debts than I had money, so I was declared bankrupt. What was open to question, though, was the amount for which I was declared bankrupt – around £350,000. I was particularly alarmed at not being invited to the meeting with the lawyers, because I knew I didn't owe that amount of money. I only had three creditors: American Express, who wanted £20,000; a tandoori restaurant in the Fulham Road, who were after £80; and the rest was supposed to be what I owed the Inland Revenue in income tax. The tax bill was ridiculous – I did still owe a little from the big-earning years, but not the bulk of it. What had happened was that for over three years nobody had been doing my accounts, so my tax liability for the years in which I hadn't earned a penny had been assessed on the last available figures – those for 1975 – during which my income was over a million pounds. It was all a gross clerical error, but because it had been allowed to get this far without being put right, in the eyes of the law I was liable for it. American Express I won't quibble with, and I probably deserved to be taken to court by them, as I had carried on using my card as often as possible after they'd told me to stop. And the tandoori restaurant never got paid back: I still go in there today, it's the same guy who owns it and I tell him that because he took me to court I'm never going to pay it – I say I'll pay the bill for whatever meal I've just eaten, but he'll never get his eighty quid. We have a good laugh about it.

The most humiliating part about being an undischarged bankrupt was having to report to the trustees every week to hand in my receipts and statements of earning and go through every little detail with them. I got pretty friendly with the people in the office, but the law said they had to go through the motions: I had to explain exactly why I booked a minicab instead of taking a bus, and convince them that I was doing everything possible to make recompense. It was a pretty pointless procedure, because it's actually ridiculous to imagine that anybody would want to remain under this jurisdiction for a minute longer than they absolutely had to. But what it meant was I *had* to work anywhere that would book me and I could no longer be at all choosy about where I played.

I had the idea that if I actually took the cabaret places seriously, and instead of doing them grudgingly went in like I was doing them a favour, I could boost my earnings – the big places were capable of paying very highly – and work my way out of this mess pretty quickly. So rather than tone my show down to suit their expectations I took rock 'n' roll, Glitter-style, to the cabaret circuit. I rehearsed with the band so we could get the old routines going; made sure I had some stairs on stage – even if it was only some crates covered with velvet; insisted that clubs had their stages raised and extended to accommodate what was going to happen; got managements to ignore noise levels; and made the audiences stand up and get involved. I could get away with the demands because I was packing places, but the only people who benefited were groups who were booked in after me because I'd left them a bigger stage, a primed audience – most people who go to these places are regulars – and less rigid management policies. I wasn't earning the money I needed, so in spite of being able to do a better job and proving I could fill five thousand-capacity venues, I still absolutely hated the places and had to get out from doing them as soon as possible. I've always told the press that I finished doing cabaret after only a few months and went straight into the universities – because I was embarrassed about it – but the truth was I stayed on that circuit for two years.

I was absolutely sick of those shows a long time before I gave them up, but as well as having to do them to satisfy the trustees I was led to believe they were my only option. As I was fairly out of it most of the time and probably feeling a bit sorry for myself, I more or less accepted this. I believed that perhaps there were no alternatives open to me in the rock or pop environment until, during that summer, in four different cities around the country I saw the same group of kids outside the venues. In their early twenties and dressed in punk fashion, they were Americans over here on holiday who were determined to see one of my shows but couldn't get in anywhere because of their clothes. I was outraged – I tried to refuse to go on at one club unless they were let in, but was advised against making such a stand or I would have been sued for ever! That's when I knew I still had something to offer the rock crowd, and asked Mike Mingard where my audience from six years previously would have been then. He told me they were in the cabaret clubs I was playing, and for the first time I thought about it and realised that couldn't be right. The arithmetic was wrong: the core of my support, ten-and eleven-year-olds who had watched me on *Top of the Pops* in 1974, were by that time only seventeen and eighteen, and much younger than the crowds I was getting at the cabaret clubs. My fans were punks now and at places like the Roxy, the Lyceum and the Music Machine – before it became the Camden Palace. I pestered Mike to make enquiries into getting one-nighters at these rock venues, and the Music Machine booked us.

When I played it they gobbed on me – apparently it was a really high accolade, but I got one straight down my throat while I was singing, and that's probably the worst thing that can happen to anybody! I felt like I was going home, though; going on stage in front of a squashed-in seething mass of kids reminded me of the early dates I'd done as Gary Glitter in the large dance halls – the same sense of danger from a tough, largely male crowd. I was sweating as much as they were. I was giving plenty to get as much back, and there was an energy coming from them that was worlds removed from the cabaret crowds, where any excitement was one-way traffic from me to them. I enjoyed that show so much that I came off feeling hot to trot, and asked Mike to get bookings in that sort of place for as many of our spare nights as he could.

We played quite a few punk venues – I don't think Mike was ever too comfortable with them, but since playing those shows was all that was keeping me from going mad he went along with it. They gobbed on me in all of them, and I had the idea of putting two wind machines on either side of the stage that I could control with a foot switch and blow it all back at them – of course, it never got past the thinking-about-it stage. Importantly, though, in spite of the fact that I was now drinking more than I ever had – it was the only way to survive the cabaret clubs – I began to feel good about what I was doing again. The punks were a new rock audience, and I could see myself starting down another trail instead of feeling like I'd definitely come to the end of one, which is the vibe I got from the other places.

I found punk very similar to Glitter in more than just its energy and air of toughness. It didn't have too much subtlety in it, which is so important if you want people just to react to the music instead of having to sit around and think about it. The followers dressed up, too, which always signifies a greater commitment than just buying tickets or records. Punk fell into place exactly with the way I was looking at life: it kicked ass, and I wanted to kick my own ass; it was anti-establishment, and I'd had a belly full of the establishment. Everything about it seemed so right for what I wanted to do that it's the only time I've ever wanted to join anybody else's gang.

But my becoming part of that gang and that gang becoming part of me was what began to get me up off the floor. And the brilliant thing about it was that you could be ugly and it didn't matter – being fat and old wasn't a handicap! The stigmas were taken away, which was exactly what we had set out to do with Glitter nearly ten years previously; all that was important was that you were there and you were doing it. Punk had an integrity and an honesty which I hadn't found much of in the showbiz world where I'd spent the last year, and I liked it.

Another episode in the later summer of 1980 not only lifted my spirits further but resulted in my getting a recording deal and mingling with the upper end of society again. The week before I played two weeks at the Golden Garter, a huge cabaret club in Manchester, I bumped into Tessa Dahl whom I knew from Tramp when I was in my heyday. She was about seventeen then and I think she quite fancied me. She still did six years later, because she sent a bunch of flowers up to the club for me – I've always loved flowers around me – and a couple of days later came up herself. She came back to the hotel and we attempted a night of passion, but one of the band set the fire alarms off and it was very much a case of coitus interruptus! Tessa stayed for the rest of the two weeks I was up there and, although we tried our hardest to have a steamy affair, all we did when we went to bed was laugh. What usually set us off was the fact that she is very tall – maybe six foot – and I'm not, and we looked pretty silly together. We definitely fell in love, even though we never became lovers in the accepted sense of the word.

Obviously Tessa knew my financial situation, and at the end of the engagement, before she went home, she told me there'd always be a bed for me at her house in London – not hers, though, she specified, as she never got any sleep through laughing too much. I took up the offer, too, and for a while she became yet another of those people who adopted me when I needed looking after. I used to go to the country with her at weekends to stay with her father, the writer Roald Dahl, and mother, the actress Patricia Neal; Patricia would call me Gary Cooper the Second, because they'd had a big affair in years gone by and she said my smile reminded her of him.

Tessa introduced me to her very jet-set circle of friends, and pretty soon I was being wined and dined and taken down to Tramp by the generation of young aristocrats below the crowd I had hobnobbed with in the seventies. They all knew I was skint, but it didn't bother them and they managed not to make me feel like a charity case. I appreciated this greatly, and it taught me a lesson that would have done me a lot of good five years before – that people were willing to accept me for who I was, and my character and charm could impress them as much as the amount of money I was willing to spend. It went a long way to helping me regain some self-respect. The irony of hanging out with this circle was that when I wasn't staying with Tessa I used to doss down on the band's guitarist's floor. He lived in Ilford, and we'd go drinking in the kind of pubs where people would offer to sell you some wheels for your car then ask you what sort of car you had! Tessa's crowd were a bit of a rabble, though – what would be termed Hooray Henrys today – and it was about this time that I got into cocaine. The drug was rife in London even though it was still fairly expensive. I began to get hooked on the stuff, because it was so freely available; and because I liked drinking so much it came in very handy – I could knock back the booze all night, and every time I felt myself getting a little woozy I'd toot up a line to straighten myself out again.

Through this social scene I got introduced to Baron Stephen Bentinck, who was twenty-four years old and had been worth £200 million from the day he was born. He was very funny actually, because he was clearly affected by the responsibilities entailed and would get very down. I still had my low moments, too, and very often Stephen and I would end up, slightly the worse for wear, crying on each other's shoulders about our predicaments – him with more dosh than he could ever spend, and me without a bean! What he did for me, though, was give me a record contract with his newly formed Eagle Records. Part of the deal was that they fixed me up with somewhere to live, so they rented a lovely mews house for me just off Brompton Road and I felt as if I was starting to get myself together – I was doing a lot of cocaine and drinking heavily, but at least I wasn't living on people's floors, so I looked at it as some kind of progression!

Stephen got me back together with Mike Leander, which he figured was the way to get the best out of me, and we recorded two singles. I'd had hardly any contact with Mike since I'd come back from Australia, and I was a bit apprehensive about going into the studio with him. It turned out fine, however, much easier than I'd feared, probably because I'd had so long to come to terms with what had happened that I no longer felt any bitterness. The records, I thought, were two of the best Glitter records ever made, 'What Your Mamma Don't See (Your Mamma Don't Know)' and 'When I'm On' – which is still in my stage set today. It was as if Mike and I had been waiting to get back together again, and once the old team was reformed the creative juices started to flow. I made my first video, too, for 'What Your Mama Don't See'. It was a bit of a disaster: I had no idea how much they cost, and I turned up four hours late simply because I'd got wrecked the night before. As the huge team of people who had been standing around for me were on hourly wages, there was very little left in the budget actually to film the clip!

That single was released in November, but it didn't sell well at all. Stephen may have had the best will in the world, but the people he employed in his promotions and marketing departments couldn't have sold a record if they'd tried. I don't think I could have, either, at that time: by then the club crowd was going for the American disco acts such as Shalamar, the Gap Band, and Earth, Wind and Fire; heavy metal had really come into its own to satisfy the essentially rock 'n' roll audience; and I couldn't hope to compete on a level with new British groups like the Jam, Madness and the Specials. David Bowie was the only act from the bunch I'd come up with that was having any contemporary success, and not enough time had passed for us to become kitsch.

In spite of its failure I did manage to finish the year convinced I still had a great deal to offer when I played the Rainbow at Finsbury Park on 20 December and packed it with a young, largely punk crowd. Johnny Rotten was there with his mum, who he brought backstage because she'd been a fan and always wanted to meet me. I took them both out to dinner at Tramp afterwards, and he's been forever grateful because she was really knocked out by the gesture. In spite of his public pose he was very impressed. He kept looking round the club and saying to me, 'I'd never be able to get in here, normally, would I?'

The Rainbow show was filmed for a video, and when I saw it played back I was staggered – I was fatter than I'd ever seen myself! I must have been gradually ballooning up over the years and not noticed, but by then I was of late Elvis proportions – another irony, as I probably had a drug habit that was roughly the equivalent, too. I was singing really well, though, and if what I look like is ignored it's a very good performance even by the seventies' standards.

'When I'm On' came out in February 1981, and sold no better than its predecessor. I wasn't that worried, however, because I knew I was getting the live side back together again, and as that's always been Glitter's foundation I knew it was just a matter of time before I built up from it. In May that year I played another big London concert. I was warned against attempting another one so soon after the Rainbow, but we went ahead and sold out the Dominion Theatre in Tottenham Court Road.

It was the same punk crowd, but by then I'd played to them so often that I started adapting my presentation to suit. I had this thing in my head about the *Spartacus* film starring Kirk Douglas, who plays the lead character who leads the slaves to revolt, and that's how I saw myself. There was mass unemployment in Britain at the time and it was separating so many of the kids from the advantages they should have had – they were dispossessed, like the slaves in that film. It was quite a visible analogy, too, as looking down from the stage their coloured Mohicans weren't unlike Roman soldiers' helmet plumes and they wore kilts similar to tunic skirts. I empathised with the punks' situation because I'd always seen myself as an outsider, and as they had by then so comprehensively adopted me I felt like their king and wanted to look like some sort of figurehead. At the Dominion I had a gladiator-style costume in purple and silver made for me – a bit showbiz, but with a few chains and studs – and decided to make my entrance in a horse-drawn chariot: I was Spartacus, and I'd arrive in triumph to lead the slaves to freedom. On reflection, the amount of drugs I was taking at the time may have had something to do with these notions, because it does sound suspiciously like a cocaine delusion – but so what? Glitter was always about being whatever you fancied yourself as!

Mike and I had real trouble getting a horse-drawn chariot for that night. We tried the BBC first, then Pinewood, and then went through every film and television contact we had until we managed to hire one from Gerry Cottle's circus. It was worth it, though, because when I made my entrance – more like Caesar than Spartacus, really – the audience went wild. Of course the horse crapped on the stage – perhaps it was a punk, too – but I was in my element. It reminded me of the night at the Palladium when I used the staircase for the first time – I was dreaming up stunts that made sure Glitter always went that little bit better, and the crowd were loving it. The reaction also opened another door for me, as Gerry Cottle had come up to watch the concert and, being such a natural showman, immediately began to see possibilities. He approached me afterwards and asked me if I'd ever considered joining the circus! I said yes, I'd *thought* about it, but no, I'd never done anything about it, because although I'd always liked the circus

I didn't understand it well enough to get involved. He told me about all the possibilities he saw for me – how I'd be able to do things that couldn't even be attempted on a regular stage, and I was hooked. Immediately.

I went down to stay at his house for a couple of days while we talked through what could be done – animals, trapezes, high wires: it was going to be fantastic! I agreed practically straightaway and Mike did the negotiations, which involved us putting up some cash we'd begged, blagged and borrowed to scrape together. I had to spend about a month learning the basics of circus performance – flying in a harness, trampolining, highwire balance (with a safety wire) and ringmaster skills, like whip cracking, which is harder than it looks. Gerry had all his lorries repainted with 'Gary Glitter's Rock 'n' Roll Circus' on the sides, and we worked out a show. Basically it was my regular stage set: my band were there and performed as part of a circus, with me as the ringmaster. I had to make about eight costume changes from my glitter ringmaster tailcoat, though, as I'd come on to perform the songs with various stunts involved. Then, while I was off, the circus performers would do their stuff. It must have looked spectacular, too: I had to trampoline over a puma in one bit; for 'Leader of the Gang' I came in suspended under a motorbike that was being ridden along a highwire – on the second night I'd had too much cocaine, got a bit excited and nearly overbalanced it; for 'Do You Wanna Touch' I made my entrance on a highwire and jumped on and off it using a trampoline; and sometimes I'd just sing as the ringmaster, with tumbling or a trapeze act going on around me.

We opened in Reading in July, and nobody came. Everybody, myself included, had been so caught up in how fabulous it was going to be that we'd overlooked too many details. The main one was that we were going for a rock crowd, but instead of the advertising being approached in rock tour terms, it was handled in the way the circus always does its publicity – handbills tacked on to trees and/or stuck in the windows of knitting wool shops or little tobacconists. There was no campaign involving large fly posters on city centre sites, or music press advertising, which are the only places rock fans get their information. Then there was the siting of the tents: circuses can get the best place in town to set up – the park in a residential area or city centre – but they operate under really stringent noise regulations because it's in a tent. So in order to present rock 'n' roll in the way it should be played we had to set up where there was nobody we could disturb, which meant outside of town. The physical touring aspect was very different too, because it takes eight hours to take down and put up a big top, so a circus can only move about fifty miles in a day, which meant – in terms of rock audience catchment areas – that we'd be playing to the same pool of people twice. All of this conspired to bring in about fifty or sixty people to a tent that had a capacity of between two and three thousand, so we only lasted three nights. We went on to play Oxford and Swindon, and held a traditional circus parade through the streets to try and drum up business – I led, and we handed out red noses. Attendances went up to a couple of hundred, but that wasn't nearly enough to stop us running out of money.

I enjoyed my time with the circus, though. I loved

the mucking-in spirit – the clown would come out and do his bit, then when he went off he'd change into a pair of overalls and carry on fixing a broken-down generator. I hired a Winnebago mobile home and lived on site with them while I was learning and during our time on the road, and made a few friends. I was personally very disappointed it had been such a failure, and often dream about trying it again – I'd like to put Gary Glitter's Rock 'n' Roll Circus on Clapham Common all through August, with me performing and presenting a different rock act every night. I'd have the animals and the performers outside all day to attract the kids, who would then make sure their mums and dads came in the evening. It would work, too, because the worst thing about the Gerry Cottle episode was that we eventually found out the demand was there all the time. The BBC had come down to make a *40 Minutes* documentary about the preparations and performance and, after it was broadcast much later in the year, Gerry's office was deluged with enquiries from people asking where it would be on and how they could get a ticket.

It was during that year I started to make headway into the university circuit. When I was doing the punk clubs, magazines like the *NME* and *Melody Maker* started to take an interest and would send people down to review the shows. As those papers have such a high student readership, social secretaries began to make enquiries. I liked these gigs because a lot of the students weren't original Glitterfans – they were either just slightly too old or too intellectual for it – but so many of them were seeing the show for the first time. The stages were always too small – at one place I punched the air and put my fist through the ceiling

– and we had to construct the steps ourselves, but the crowds were always very supportive. Even though I was convinced we could have done more to exploit the universities, by the end of the year we had added enough of them to the clubs we were doing to be able to leave cabaret behind at last.

I got a record deal towards the end of that year too, at Bell. I hooked up with Mike Leander on it: we had the idea of getting me to record an album of cover versions which were traditionally girls' songs, but we'd change the lyrics from 'he' to 'she' and vice versa. It was to have a lot of strings on it which Mike was to arrange, but he didn't come back from Majorca in time for the sessions. I did them with another arranger, but it didn't turn out the way I wanted it to and only one single ever got released. 'And Then She Kissed Me' just scraped into the Top 40, but the company didn't pick up any further option on me, which was a shame because any chart placing at all was better than I'd had for a long time. I think that was the final straw for Mike Mingard, because in early 1982 he told me he no longer wanted to manage me. It didn't come as a great surprise, because he'd become less and less involved with the day-to-day running of my professional life since the circus – he was increasingly leaving it up to Alan Gee, the guy who'd originally been taken on as my driver and was now effectively my tour manager. I think the financial fiasco of the circus had caused him to lose heart, and it was just a case of things getting too much for him – it didn't really matter how profitable he made me then because so much had to go to the receiver. I wasn't really that sorry, either, as we didn't see eye to eye about Gary Glitter's role in the 1980s: Mike Mingard was convinced it was purely a nostalgia trip, but I wanted the opposite – to play on the old days, but to take them beyond nostalgia into a contemporary setting, like I've done with the Gang Show now.

My biggest worry was being managerless; Alan stayed with me and did his best, but he didn't have the skills or the contacts to be effective from a business point of view. So it came as quite a relief when Lawrence Meyers – the accountant who had set up GTO ten years previously – offered to manage me. I'd kept in contact with Lawrence since my return, and he and his wife always treated me like one of the family. They were lovely people, and every time I got really low I'd ring him up and say, 'Can I come and stay at your house tonight, because it's nice there?' I figured it wasn't so wrong of me to impose myself on him occasionally, because he used to take great delight in telling people that Gary Glitter paid for his house and David Bowie paid for his yacht! He still owns the master tapes of all the big Glitter hits, and probably a few of Bowie's as well. After GTO had ceased operations in the seventies he'd gone into the film business as a producer, and used to take me to Cannes every year just to cheer me up. It really did too, because we'd stay at the Carlton Hotel and I'd get the full luxury treatment. It would remind me, too, that I was still newsworthy, because when I walked through the lobby the huge UK press corps down there would be on me like a shot! That was the most amusing part of my low years – even though I was broke, I was still very famous. One year, when The Who were playing a concert just outside Cannes, I went as a VIP and met David Essex backstage. He hadn't done so well in 1981 and 1982, and he pulled me to one side and asked me what direction I thought he should take in his career. I was staggered, I hadn't got two pennies to rub together and he was asking me for advice! But that was the essence of Glitter – to stand there, champagne in hand, blagging your way through life.

Lawrence's film business wasn't doing so well, however – in spite of one of his productions being the Anthony Quinn film *The Greek Tycoon* – and he wanted to get back into the music industry. As with returning to anything after being away for several years, though, he'd found that things had moved on. He couldn't just walk into record companies and blag deals any more, because his contacts from a decade earlier were no longer there, and their replacements had their own Lawrence Meyerses to do deals with. He thought that a good way back in would be with me, as he knew me, and I was glad of his offer because he wanted to put things on a very businesslike footing. Everything had to pay: there'd be no more flakey ventures like running away with the circus or spending £2,000 in hotel bills to do a show that paid us £1,500 – if we couldn't turn a guaranteed profit, he didn't want to know. That was exactly what I needed – somebody to act like a bank – and the first thing Lawrence did was get me signed with the Derek Block Agency, who handled acts like Tears for Fears, UB40 and Duran Duran. That wasn't an organisation with which I was too happy to get involved, however, because I'd heard a lot of rumours about it not being entirely straight with its clients; while these rumours might have been just gossip, they made me wary. But Jef Hanlon, whom I'd known for years and trusted implicitly, had gone to Derek Block when he left RAM, so I agreed on condition that I was handled solely by him.

Lawrence and Jef immediately saw the potential in the universities, which seemed to be starved of good rock acts – anybody who was experienced enough to put on a good show was too big to bother with them. During 1982 they put together two thirty- or forty-date tours of universities, with a few rock clubs in there as well, the second of which took us well into 1983. I had another stab at recording during 1982 when Ian Marsh and Martyn Ware of Heaven 17 approached me to take part in their BEF album *Music of Quality and Distinction*. Their idea was to get their pop heroes to sing whatever covers they fancied and it would come out as a compilation – Tina Turner, Sandie Shaw and Paul Jones were also on it. I recorded 'Suspicious Minds' and 'Be My Baby', which were a lot of fun to do, but they weren't at all successful as singles and the album didn't sell that well either – it was too personal for the general public.

Unfortunately, in the summer of 1983 Lawrence discovered that in spite of his plans for maximising my earnings we'd lost money. Although the universities were selling out they were expensive to do, because they were not carefully routed tours, and our travelling costs had been astronomical. It was enough to convince him he couldn't get back into the music business and he decided to return to films. I was rather upset we couldn't make a success of it, because Lawrence was a good friend. I remained with Jef at the Derek Block Agency, though, and it was a situation that was about to restart my career in earnest. With a little help from Rod Stewart.

12
Home and Dry

During the summer of 1983, through the Derek Block Agency, Jef was booking the European leg of Rod Stewart's world tour and put me on as support at the shows at Versailles in France and Glasgow's Ibrox Park. The French show I didn't enjoy at all – the audience only knew 'Rock 'n' Roll, Part 1' and it was obvious all through my set that they were only waiting for Rod. It didn't inspire me, and I didn't perform very well. Ibrox promised to be a different matter, though, and represented a smart move on Jef's part. Right from the very beginning Glasgow's always been a Glitter stronghold, probably because it's such a tough city, and there's always been a crossover between Rod's and my fan bases. It was an ideal opportunity for me to prove to a huge audience, the country's media and the industry at large that I had a lot to offer, and it would also give Rod's fans extra value for money.

I was hesitant when Jef told me he wanted me to play there, however, as I hadn't done many stadium shows – it's a different way of doing things from a university. All the gestures and patter have to be very exaggerated, and of course I couldn't borrow Wembley to rehearse! I felt I was on home territory up there, though – I was coming hot from the universities, and if I turned it down I'd never get another offer like it. So I agreed. However, the show in Versailles hadn't done anything to make me feel easier about it, and in spite of Rod doing his best to talk me up in radio interviews – he drove home the point that I was the hardest act to follow – I was very nervous.

I thought it would do us good to get into the part of big rock stars playing stadiums and we arrived in style to psyche ourselves up: we had the best possible coach we could hire and had booked into a top hotel. It definitely worked as an ego-boost, but the amusing thing was that we'd had to leave London a day early and play Durham University on the way to Glasgow to get the money to pay for it all!

It was a glorious summer day. Rod's set was completely white and the crowd of 29,000 on the pitch was a sea of blue and white Scottish flags, cut practically in half by a long white catwalk that extended out from the stage; if there is such a thing as a perfect setting for a gig, this was it. When I went out to do my set I was given instructions not to use the catwalk. Apparently Rod – who hadn't arrived yet because he never does until ten minutes before he has to go on – had insisted that I left it for him. However, the Glasgow audience were with me 100 per cent of the way. I couldn't put a foot wrong and, although I fully intended to comply with Rod's wishes, as my confidence started to soar I began eyeing up this catwalk every time I passed it. In the end I couldn't ignore it any longer, and when I finished with 'Leader of the Gang' I took a flying leap on to the catwalk and ran to the end to stand with my arms up in triumph. The crowd went absolutely crazy, but when I tried to get back on stage for the big finish I couldn't. It was about a four-foot step. I found out later that Rod has a little white trampoline that nobody can see, but of course that hadn't been put there yet and I was stuck! So I finished the set down there and then, because I couldn't think of anything else to do, I ran back to the end of it, punched the air a couple more times and collapsed. The fans nearest the catwalk threw so many Scottish flags on me that I couldn't stand for the weight of them. Three roadies carried me off, still stretched out.

It was the kind of finale I couldn't have planned if I'd thought about it for a year, and at that moment I thought 'I'm back!' It had nothing to do with hit records or money or media attention – it was simply the way 29,000 people had shown how much they cared for me, and in turn I had responded by giving one of my best performances ever. If ever there was a rock 'n' roll statement, this was it: I was in a stadium, going for it in front of a rock audience that was fighting for me and fighting with me. *Everybody* was together, and I knew then that, whatever obstacles I might yet have to get over, the Gang was out there, I was the Leader, and Glitter still had its strength. Rod was very good about the incident too: he hadn't been there when it happened, and when I saw him as he was going on he asked, 'You used it, didn't you?' I nodded and he just smiled and said, 'I knew I couldn't keep you off it in Glasgow!'

Rod had turned in an extra-special performance after that – he knew he had to – and that wee night it was as if Glasgow belonged to us. We went out to a club, but neither of us enjoyed ourselves because we had to have too many minders around, so we went back to the hotel to make merry in Rod's suite. I can't remember if I got back to my suite or not; I think I dossed on his sofa, but whatever happened I missed our coach back to London. Jef took me down to the airport with Rod's party, but we were told the flight was absolutely full. It was by then pouring with rain, so Jef appealed to the girl behind the desk, saying he had to get this guy back to London because if he was left out in this weather he'd go rusty. The girl asked who it was, and when Jef replied 'Gary Glitter' suddenly the ticket was issued and I travelled down on one of the stewardesses' folding seats! It was another little reminder that I had a strong following out there.

Rod's next show was in Dublin, and because we were enjoying ourselves so much he invited me to come along. I went on the condition he lent me some socks when I got there – which I haven't given back to him and I still wear. What, in effect, he'd done was to manipulate a situation that would completely ensure my return as a serious rock music contender. I didn't find out until much later, that he had made sure I sat next to Jef on the plane, and had told Jef to try and sort something out with a view to looking after my affairs. It's such a short flight that we didn't have time to get into a serious discussion, but we were both keen and agreed to talk further when we were back in London. Although it was an obvious solution to my managerlessness, neither of us would have thought of it without Rod's intervention. Another thing that Rod did for me on that trip was offer to put up money if I was to go into the recording studio: he'd promised that for every pound I could raise towards the costs he'd match it with a pound of his own. I didn't take him up on the offer, but his making it was one of the most moving things that had ever happened to me. Not simply because of its generosity, but because it was so thoughtful – it wasn't merely a handout, as I had to raise money first. I had to get off my backside and help myself, which was exactly what I needed. I am still indebted to Rod for what he did for me then – it was even more than he'd tried to do for me back in the seventies. Rod Stewart genuinely is one of life's gentlemen.

At the show in Dublin, Jef and I got very drunk on tequila and Rod brought me out to sing 'Sailing' with him, which sent the place into a frenzy. Again the public had made me feel like a star, but before the show I'd done something to make myself feel like one. At the hotel an Irish TV crew were waiting to interview Rod, but he was getting a lot of grief from his wife Alana at the time and was holed up in his suite on the phone to London. They were getting very near to deadline and decided if they couldn't get to Rod they'd interview me about what it's like being Rod's best mate. Jef told them it would cost them – I think the exact words he used were: 'Mr Glitter has overheads to consider'! The camera crew had a quick whip round, scraped together £50 and gave it to me, I did the interview and then walked into the bar, where Rod's band were waiting, and shouted, 'Barman! Champagne for my friends!' and blew the lot. It was such a brilliant feeling – one I hadn't had since 1980 because I hadn't been allowed any money. I couldn't have been more certain that I had turned the corner for good.

Soon afterwards Jef became my manager, and devised a two-year deal which guaranteed me a living and, so we believed, would allow him to start straightening out my finances: against a percentage of the net take he rented a flat for me to live in, paid all the utilities for me and gave me £200 per week for personal expenses; he also agreed to provide a band and sound equipment for my show. In return I had to be available to work for him 365 nights a year. It was a wonderful arrangement for my peace of mind, because I knew I'd have somewhere to live for two years, and although the £200 was the absolute maximum Jef could get past the receiver it was enough for me to buy clothes, eat out and generally feel like a human being again. It was in his interest to build my career, too, and we took it from there.

Thanks to Jef's skills as a booking agent and promoter, by the end of 1983 I was undisputed king of the university circuit – there was even an article in *The Times* called 'Glitter On Campus'! I'd sell out everywhere I went; in that period I sold out three nights at Norwich within an hour of the tickets going on sale, which was unheard-of business. It was very much a personal victory for me too, because when I first started playing colleges I was well aware of the fact that I was a novelty act for the Christmas Ball. In the beginning students would come along to the shows with the attitude, 'Let's get out of our heads and give it some seventies with old Gazza – take the piss!' But before long I'd won them over to such an extent and they felt so certain they'd have a good time at one of my shows that they couldn't get enough of it. And I put a lot of effort into making sure they'd have an evening to remember. While I was establishing myself

I traded on the fact that people weren't too fussy, and experimented with my act until I'd honed it to perfection. It was much like the way I'd worked on it in Germany and I knew exactly how to get particular responses from the crowds, so that by 1983 they were as well trained in their parts as the Gang had ever been. And they loved every minute of it.

I believe it was playing the universities at this time and having the opportunity to redevelop my act for a mainstream audience – as opposed to the punks – that gave me the grounding for the Gang Show in years to come. I'm sure that if I hadn't done those colleges I would never have ended up at Wembley years later. Also, those virtually captive campus audiences provided the means for survival until I could move up a notch. That was because the music business is a lottery – even the young hip bands with precisely the right haircut aren't guaranteed to last, so at that stage of my career I couldn't count on anything. Except in the universities. There I'd become so much a part of college life – Gary Glitter at the Fresher Ball or the end-of-term knees-up – I knew I would always be working, so I could hang on in there until something broke.

As 1984 came around we were strong enough to start adding the occasional concert hall to the colleges, so instead of doing the local university we'd book ourselves into somewhere like Victoria Hall in Hanley – and nearly fill it, too. Then, early in the new year, I had another go at America. I'd never been quite able to swallow the disappointment of what had happened to me in the States. The most demoralising aspect was that I felt I'd never been given the chance, even though I'd had a massive hit in that country: first there were the club dates that Mike Leander ducked out of doing; then the laughable PR trips; and finally the debacle with Clive Davis. I felt I was still a long way from giving the USA my best shot. Every British rock 'n' roller wants to play it to the Americans – not just for the huge money that can be earned, but because acknowledgement from where it all began is like getting an official seal of approval.

We were riding high in Britain, and as the demand went up from the universities so did our fees. Jef was taking care of that end of it well enough to get the money together to take a band over to America for some shows, so we were just waiting for the right opportunity. At the beginning of 1984 I had a greatest hits album out called *The Leader*, which was doing quite well in the UK on the back of my live successes. Since Epic Records in New York wanted to put it out we figured this would be the right time to do a small tour over there – just half a dozen clubs around New York, Chicago and Detroit, to give the album a push. Jef arranged an agent for us over there, and the first show we played was the opening of the Limelight club in New York – I'd been specifically requested for that because the girl who did the PR was English, and had been in the Gang since the seventies. It was an excellent night: I was astonished at the number of American kids who turned up with Glitter records for me to sign; and there was a great deal of support from people in the industry – Little Steven, Carly Simon, Ronnie Wood, Ronnie Ramone and Dr John were there.

Already I was feeling good about America – the first time I'd felt like I was in control of things and going the best I could over there. When we went up to do a club in Boston I was astonished as I stepped on stage to hear the audience chanting: 'Leader! Leader!' It turned out that nearly everybody in the place was Scottish – they all worked in the local fishing industry, because the money was better than back home! We really enjoyed ourselves that night and felt this was turning into a dream trip, but from then on it started to go wrong. Next night we were in Poughkeepsie, New York State, in one of the weirdest situations I'd ever been in – the club had a massive stage and a really tiny area for the audience, I was on a bill with Steppenwolf, the Band and Paul Young, and there were only two customers in the place! By the time we went back down to New York I was getting worried because I'd not seen the record anywhere – it turned out Epic had put the release date back four weeks and not bothered to tell us. We were spending £20,000 that could have gone towards my bankruptcy discharge trying to promote a record that nobody could buy! I put all the Glitter gear on, stormed into the record company executive's daily breakfast meeting with a big bag of bagels, introduced myself, told them why I was in their city and suggested they try and force the bagels into an alternative orifice! Unsurprisingly, that was the last contact I ever had with them, and the record had no promotional push from them when it did eventually come out.

Chicago was cancelled because we couldn't risk any more money. I was very disappointed, because that city had been so good to me that I really wanted to play there. I went down very well in Detroit, though – another tough city – which was my first show before ordinary Americans. I knew enough about audiences to know, from reading that crowd, that America would have wanted what we had to offer; if we had had a bit of record company support and some product out while we were there, we could have given it to them. One day I'm going to get there.

Back in Britain that summer I put out my first single for eighteen months, 'Dance Me Up', which got to Number 25 and put me on *Top of the Pops*. That was quite funny, because I hadn't been there for nine years and it was exactly the same – a lot of the technicians were still those who had given me a hard time in the seventies. I didn't feel particularly misty-eyed about going back there, because the one change they had made I thought had taken the spirit out of it: they used canned applause at the beginning and end of the numbers, so because the kids no longer got worked up the atmosphere was flat. I did the song with Mike Leander, who had cut himself a deal with Arista Records on one of their sub-labels that was owned by Dick Leahy, who ran Bell Records UK when we were with them in the seventies. Mike had written the tune and Eddie Seago the lyrics, and they needed somebody like myself to front it. As there never has been anybody quite like myself, he asked me to do it. I agreed simply because I liked the song and felt the timing was right for me to release a new record. Besides, it was another couple of steps up on the long climb back, and I'm sure if I'd said no Mike would have got somebody else to do it.

It brought Mike and me back together again, and regardless of what I might have felt personally I knew he was the only writer/producer I'd ever had hits with – that still stands today. Because I was so satisfied with my live work I was eager to see if I could translate that into record sales, and the success of 'Dance Me Up' seemed to indicate I could. We wanted to do an album, but Arista only wanted to commit to another single because they obviously weren't sure about me. We fought and we won, but that situation was absolutely typical of the industry's attitude towards me. I was selling as many tickets as we could get printed, I'd just had a hit, but the record company was unwilling to back me with any muscle. When I did *Top of the Pops* the industry raised its eyebrows and asked where I'd sprung back up from, only thinking of me as some irritant that wouldn't go away. I was still the outsider, and I've yet to understand why the business refuses to accept that I have public approval. If we'd had a major company willing to take us seriously at that time, I would have got to where I am today much, much quicker.

In September, on a blazing hot day, we wrote 'Another Rock 'n' Roll Christmas'. Eddie Seago came in to help us because we had just twelve days to do a whole album on a pitiful budget of £25,000 (that's how seriously Arista took us), but it was as if we'd turned the clock back more than a decade – bizarrely, the studio we were in was owned by one of the original Glitterband. The flow got going, I told the others I had a good title, 'Another Rock 'n' Roll Christmas', Eddie added the line 'Another Christmas rock 'n' roll' and we built the song up from there. It didn't surprise me at all that it was a Top 10 hit, because it was Mike and me working how we worked best – completely instinctively. The only trouble was we were both drinking too much, and whereas I'd have a toot to bring me back he didn't touch anything like that and after three or four hours he'd be out of it. The album

Boys Will Be Boys came out early the next year and was very good. It didn't sell too badly either, but Arista still dropped the option on our contract.

By 1985 we were earning huge money from the universities, and Jef decided that this was to be the year I got out from under the bankruptcy. He took advice and approached the trustees, offering to make a deal. He'd gone into all the ins and outs of the tax I was supposed to have owed and had the documentation to prove that, in spite of the court judgement, the amount was far in excess of what I should have paid – this is something Mike Mingard should have done at the original hearing, but probably never thought of. American Express had been paid by now and the Inland Revenue were willing to settle. It cost us all we had and a little more besides, but we knew we could earn it back and at last I was discharged.

What I didn't realise was how quickly I'd recoup it – during the later part of that summer, when I did a Heinz soup TV advert, we got back everything we'd given the receiver. It wasn't the first time we'd been approached, as I had a high profile in advertising agencies as a result of the university tours: most of the bright young creative talent in the agencies – twenty-three– and twenty-four-year-olds – had been at university during the previous four years. As I'd played almost every college in the country most of them had seen me, and a lot of them were now in the Gang. I'd performed at two or three advertising awards dinners and at a couple of the larger agencies' Christmas parties. The youngsters looked upon me as a metaphor for the seventies, and every time they needed to portray an aging raver they'd get on the phone to Jef. We'd turned them all down up until then, because there was a definite stigma about doing commercials – it's a bit like appearing on *Seaside Special*. The only way we could be persuaded to agree to one was to have a large creative input so it could be kept rock 'n' roll and didn't portray me as a has-been. This particular agency, however, brought me in from the very beginning, and the guy in charge of the project, Terry Lovelock, had also done the Joan Collins/Leonard Rossiter Cinzano adverts as well as the 'refreshes the parts other beers cannot reach' campaign, so I knew he was the best. We hit it off instantly, and between us we came up with the shoes and shoulders idea for the advert, which was how most people thought of me.

I didn't have a record contract at the time, so I was missing out on all the promotion that goes with a record release, but that advert was better than having a hit. It was on television, which is a far stronger marketplace than radio; the joke contained in it allowed people to see me as a character instead of just a performer; and it was on all the time – until I had this vested interest I'd never paid attention to TV adverts and so had no idea they were shown so frequently. During October and November it was virtually impossible to switch on without seeing Gary Glitter.

This exposure immediately translated itself into ticket sales for the Christmas shows: our fees went up, we were able to spend more money on the staging, and for the first time we could slot in venues like the Birmingham Odeon, the Manchester Apollo and Hammersmith Palais and be sure of selling them out.

In February 1986 I moved out of London, which was a great relief. I had desperately missed living in the country simply because I like to be able to walk anonymously, which I couldn't do around my London flat in West Hampstead because the advert had made me as recognisable as in the seventies. There were other reasons, too: I was using all sorts of illegal substances and the crowd I was mixing with were as heavily involved as I was – there was speed and coke around me all the time, and I was getting hooked. Although I can't remember making a conscious decision to clean myself I know I suspected I was getting in too deep, so a different environment would get a lot of quite dangerous people off my back. Also, now I was enjoying some success I felt obliged to go on the star trip again and start visiting the clubs and restaurants I had gone to in my heyday. But I couldn't afford that lifestyle yet, so if I got out of London there was the added advantage that I wouldn't have to make so many excuses for not going out.

The other consideration was also financial. For the £300 a week I was paying for my flat in London I could rent a lovely house in the country. Added to which, having just got my driving licence back it was now actually possible for me to live out of town.

I rented a cottage in Bampton, near Swindon, but it didn't turn out to be a particularly happy move for me. My biggest disappointment was that my girlfriend didn't move in with me – I was then very much in love with a girl whom I'd known for five years. I met Alison in the summer of 1980, just after I'd been declared bankrupt and was emotionally and physically very low. I had nowhere to live and was on the road as much as possible because it meant I slept in a hotel bed instead of on somebody's floor. I was playing a Friday and Saturday at the Webbington Country Club

near Weston-Super-Mare, and she was at the first
night with her mum and dad. At that time I used to
bring a girl up on stage to sing 'Oh Yes, You're
Beautiful' to, and since she looked stunning that
evening I picked her. Afterwards, I thought no more
about it. The next day there was a message left for me
at the Country Club reception saying that the girl who
had come up on stage and her family would like to
meet me. They came over, we chatted and I found out
she was only fifteen years old. I was amazed, as she
looked at least five years older. Pauline, Alison's
Mum, told me they would be at the show again that
night, but before they left she invited me to come to
their house in Weston-Super-Mare for Sunday lunch.
That really touched me – it's not the sort of thing
people normally say to somebody famous. Also, I was
having such a bad time with life in general that I
figured I needed something like that.

I spent a wonderful afternoon with them because
they were such charming people. I realised I'd
forgotten what it was like to sit down and have a big
home-cooked meal in a family situation – they
bickered and teased each other, with no airs and
graces, and I felt part of a natural warmth I hadn't
experienced since I was six years old in Banbury. I
literally basked in it, and stayed for five days.

During that Sunday afternoon Pauline told me that
Alison had been a huge Glitter fan in the seventies
when she was eight and nine, and then showed me her
bedroom – it was completely papered, the ceiling as
well, with pictures of me. I was staggered. I'd heard
about people doing this, but I'd never seen it because
I'd never been into a fan's house before. It was a
genuinely mind-blowing experience to stand there and

see the care and love and attention that had gone into that collection: as well as the pictures, she had all the records in pristine, polished condition, together with scrapbooks devoted to me that had been beautifully put together. I was absolutely lost for words, because up until then I'd always thought of fans in the plural, as a huge group that came to the shows. I'd never thought about them as individuals who not only got so much from me but were prepared to give so much back in time and care like Alison had. That might sound arrogant, but I don't believe any celebrity thinks any other way. It made me feel I had a responsibility. I have got to pull myself out of this slump, I thought. For that girl. I believed I owed it to her and all the others like her.

When I arrived back in London I was bubbling, as those five days had revitalised me in mind and spirit. I felt pretty good physically after the rest and the home cooking, and I was raring to start my planned rebuilding process. I phoned Alison's Mum and Dad to thank them, and they invited me down again – I'd been honest with them about the state I was in, and they told me to come down any time I felt particularly low. I took them up on that offer many times, and their household became the nearest thing I had to a home at that time.

The feelings Alison and I had for each other developed over the years. Although I knew I was falling in love with her I was very aware of her age and made sure things didn't move too fast – I didn't go to bed with her until four years after we'd met. Her emotions for me became stronger over that period too, because after she had come to terms with me as a person rather than as her pop star idol she began to care deeply for me. Once while I was staying there I became very ill – it was the result of taking too much speed and then stopping taking it, and I was going cold turkey. I felt as if I had a bad dose of flu: I was sweating hot and cold, shaking and near-delirious. Alison slept on the floor beside me and held my hand all night, because she thought I was going to die. She had seen me at my very worst, which was not pleasant, and was still there – so I knew we had something special going between us.

The reason I had chosen Bampton to live when I moved to the country was because it was almost exactly halfway between Weston-Super-Mare and London, and I had assumed that Alison would move in with me. She didn't, I found out much later that this was simply because I didn't actually ask her to. However, her Mum was also worried about Gary Glitter's reputation – which was still much bigger than Paul Gadd's reality – and thought I was jumping into bed with women all over the place. At the time I felt very let down when Alison remained at home as I felt it was important for both of us, and for our relationship, that we lived together. I definitely would have cleaned up much sooner than I did. I was fairly resentful about it, and threw myself into life in the village, whose social scene revolved around the pub. If I wasn't in it, then it came back to my house with me: on Sundays my son Paul, now in his twenties, would bring his bass guitar and we'd sing rock-a-billy in the pub at lunchtime. When they threw everyone out at about four o'clock I'd bring the population of both bars back to my place to carry on until the pub opened again; then at around midnight they'd come back with me for a late drink! It was a silly time.

One Sunday I'd played Reading University the night before, had an all-night booze-up afterwards and then gone to the village pub for the lunchtime session. Then when I got home at six I got a phone call from my Australian friend David Ginges and his wife Bronwyn, who were in Vienna en route for London and said they'd both love to see me. I had a little nap, a hair of the dog and got in the car to drive to Heathrow, practically legless after nearly twenty-four hours of solid drinking. It was daft really, because I had plenty of money to get a cab, and when I was driving through Bicester in Oxfordshire I got pulled.

It was awful, because I was taken to the police station where they wouldn't let me out for several hours – I was ranting and raving at them, which didn't please them at all. I'd only just got my licence back after the last ban, too, and I remembered the arguments I'd had with Jef before he'd get me a car – quite rightly, he didn't trust me – and thought what a waste of time it had been. I knew I was going to get another ban, but this time I was really terrified because it was my third offence; under those circumstances a custodial sentence is customary.

A few days later I had no gigs to do for a couple of nights, Paul had gone home, David and Bronwyn were in London sight-seeing and I was alone. I was very worried about the court case and thought if I could just get some sleep I'd be able to think clearer in the morning. So I took some sleeping pills. With all the speed and coke I was doing they didn't have much effect, so I took some more. Then, what often happens is the pills start working, you get a bit woozy and forget you've taken them. So I took some more.

I woke up in the Radcliffe Infirmary in Oxford, having had my stomach pumped out. I was later told that I'd phoned Paul and sounded so out of it he'd driven down from London in the middle of the night and taken me to hospital.

That incident has frequently been reported as a suicide attempt, but it wasn't. Others have said that it was a dodge I pulled to keep out of prison. That's not true either – because of the amount of uppers I was using, I probably would have killed myself trying to take enough to make it look convincing. Purely and simply, it was an accident. But the reaction from the music world was fantastic: I came home to find my house entirely filled with flowers, sent by Elton; Rod sent a message, as did David Essex and Eric Clapton, and the sentiment was the same from all of them – 'Don't ever let yourself get that far down the line that you do something like that again.' But I hadn't. I didn't do it on purpose.

I went to court a few weeks later and got a ten-year ban and a £2,000 fine; I was remanded on bail for psychiatric reports before the magistrates made up their minds whether or not to send me to jail. Both the court-appointed doctor and an independent psychiatrist wrote letters stating that my mental state was so fragile that to put me in prison would be devastating. Fortunately the magistrates saw fit not to give me a custodial sentence, but prior to that court appearance jail seemed so close that I practically had my toothbrush packed. Of course I was happy that I didn't get put away, but these reports really drove home to me what a bad way I was in. I thought about them and the wealth of goodwill from people that followed the overdose, and knew I had to change. The

first thing I did was move. It was too easy to drink fa.
too much in Bampton – ironic, really. I'd moved from
London to get away from the drug crowd, and now
had to leave the village I'd moved to because I had
the pub in my front room all the time!

I thought I would move close to my Uncle John
because he's the closest thing I'd ever had to a father
figure. I got a beautiful house in Wroxton, near
Banbury, and decided to try to go back to my roots.
I couldn't, though, or rather what I was looking for
wasn't there – since my grandmother had died in 1959
everybody except John had moved away, and I'd been
gone so long I didn't know anybody. It was a very
painful experience, because in my mind it was the
same place it was when I was a child, yet when I got
there it had changed so much I felt almost as if my
early life had been taken away from me. I was further
away from Alison, too, and because I could no longer
drive I couldn't be independent and had to rely on
John and his wife Sally for everything. That particularly depressed me, and the peace and quiet I had
been looking for became like enforced solitude. I felt
very cut off.

I was convinced that Alison was having an affair, as
well, because suddenly I saw much less of her. I
invited her to come up to stay one weekend when I
intended to find out the truth, but again I got
absolutely wrecked. This period was probably the
peak of my drug abuse. I had the physical pressure of
playing regularly, with all that that involved, and I
also had money to spend on cocaine – I'd get through
roughly fifteen grams of coke and ten grams of speed
a week. But this weekend I set new records. I'd been
drinking and tooting all day Saturday, and because

Alison was behaving strangely with me I thought there was somebody else. Up until then our relationship hadn't been too physical, because she lived at home and I was always on the road, but I did expect her to stay overnight with me in Wroxton. The next day, for some reason, I was on a Mandrax bender and asked her if there was another man. In my drug-crazed state I was convinced there was, so I said, 'Come on then, let's go out to lunch to celebrate!' I was very out of it. We went to the Wroxton House Hotel where I drank two bottles of champagne by myself and was full of sarcastically false bonhomie – it was all bravado, because inside I was completely torn apart.

I know I spent the whole meal taunting her, but I don't remember going home from there. When we got back I was half asleep from the pills and pissed out of my brains, and I started physically threatening her. I think I hit her, but I'm sure I didn't mean to; I think it was a threat that went too far. I felt so terrible about it that I ran out of the house and into the fields and collapsed. When I returned after a few hours. Alison had gone. She'd phoned Uncle John and told him I'd flipped, so he'd taken her back to his house where she waited for her father to pick her up.

I was utterly overwhelmed by what I'd done, because the only time I'd ever raised my hand to a woman was to Victoria years ago in Germany, and was very deeply hurt that I'd lost Alison in such a terrible way. So I went on a bender – a bender of frightening proportions. I haven't a clue what I actually took, because I took everything I could find in the house. I think the only reason I stopped was because I'd cleaned out every one of my secret stashes

– and in those days I used to buy in bulk. Then on the following Sunday there was a large piece in the *News of the World*'s magazine *Sunday* about me.

Alison had been so distraught after realising what I had become – I really had turned into some sort of monster – that she wrote an article for that paper describing exactly the condition I'd descended to. She was obviously so hurt by what had happened that she wanted to hit out at me as hard as possible, and after having been with me for so long she was much more aware than most people of the power the press had over me.

I began to read it, but because of the state I was still in didn't realise the article was actually about me. I kept coming back to it, reading it a bit more carefully each time, until slowly it began to dawn on me exactly what I was reading. My first reaction was one of disbelief – I just ranted and raved about what rubbish it all was, but somewhere in the back of my mind I knew Alison cared deeply about me – quite regardless of whether she had another boyfriend or not – and that she wasn't a person who could be malicious. Eventually it started to sink in that every word of it was true – I really was a drug-addled maniac. The full force of that truth hit me so hard I literally couldn't stand up. I was in my kitchen where I sank on to my knees and ended up lying on the tiled floor.

I refuse to believe that a human being's self-esteem can sink any lower than mine reached after reading that article, written by a woman who had once held my hand all night because she thought I was going to die. And when it hits those depths, something cracks inside. Or it may genuinely have been an act of God.

But I could not get up off that kitchen floor. I lay there for ten days. I pissed there, I crapped there, I slept there and I lay awake there. The only time I moved was to get the occasional drink of water, and then I had to drag myself physically across the floor and haul myself up by clinging on to the sink to reach the taps. I couldn't stand up at all: it wasn't that I'd lost the use of my legs, but I felt as though I had an enormous weight pressing down on me that I simply couldn't lift. I tried, but I couldn't shift myself. And I was scared. Tremblingly scared. Not because I couldn't get off the floor, but scared of what I might encounter if I did. After I'd been down there a few days I stopped fighting it, because I felt safe down there. The kitchen floor was like a sanctuary: as long as I stayed down there nobody could hurt me and I could cause no pain to other people.

It was an absolutely horrible state to be in, and even five years later it still gives me the shakes just to think about it. I can only assume that I was having some kind of nervous breakdown, and with nobody there to do anything about it I had to come to terms with it myself. I began to feel that down there I had a piece of the planet that was mine, and if I wanted any more I had to get it a little piece at a time. Maybe two drinks of water a day instead of one and very gradually build up to getting back to life. During the last couple of days on the floor I felt the weight slowly lift and then, over a period of about twenty-four hours, I pushed myself up into a standing position.

It wasn't over at that point, either. Once I started moving round the house I still had to take it a bit at a time. One day venture into the garden, the next go for a walk in the lane, then have a run. It was the same with eating: at first something very light, then building up to full meals. What was happening, I think, was that I was being mentally reborn. Not in any blinding flash of light or religious sense of the word, but somewhere in the depths of my despair my brain had blown a few fuses and was now putting the circuits back together properly. Because I was reconditioning my whole approach to life, my thinking was undergoing a fundamental change, yet I wasn't doing it consciously. I didn't sit down and plan a new way of life; I just started living one. I can't understand how it happened, and to this day I do not know the reason why I couldn't get up off that kitchen floor.

I totally cleaned up my act. Since then I haven't taken another drink, or any drugs other than prescribed medication. I didn't try and cut down gradually, because I've always been so all-or-nothing about everything in life that the only way I'd be able to stop would be to cut it out completely. What surprised me most was how easy it was now that I'd made my mind up. One of the excuses for not stopping that I'd been making to myself for years was that I wouldn't be able to stand the withdrawals. At that time, though, I got into running and working out. I found that going for a run and really pushing myself released enough adrenalin to combat any discomfort I was experiencing from not taking speed any more, and it gave me a natural high. It took a few months, but I managed to reinvent myself as a human being. Or rather as Paul Gadd, also known as Gary Glitter, instead of wondering when I ought to take off the stage character. Once I'd stepped off the escalating cycle of drugs and drink I found I could be myself, and both I and others could get a kick out of what I had to offer. There was no longer any need to be 'on' all the time.

I found I could perform without stimulants, too. For the first time since the Star Club I was totally aware of what I was doing on stage and was loving every minute of it. I was getting fitter and so I could perform better. I was able to take more chances in the act: before, a big worry had been that the speed would stop me feeling pain, so I was always scared I'd injure myself without realising it.

The new me seemed to inspire the whole band, and as 1986 turned into 1987 we went on the road with the best performances since the seventies – or perhaps even better than in our heyday.

I had to get myself together so drastically because I knew I'd betrayed the trust of everybody who had given me a chance to prove once more what I could do. I worried a great deal about letting Rod down, because he'd helped me in the seventies and offered to get me started in America when he went; then more recently, too, it was thanks to him that I had got back on the trail. Jef cooled to me completely after my breakdown. He was my manager, but it was Alan Gee who dealt with me on a day-to-day basis, and so I don't think Jef knew the extent of my problem. The reality of it shocked him and he felt – quite rightly – that I'd thrown all the hard work he'd done back in his face. Of course there was Alison too, whom I felt even worse about by then because she'd been so worried about me after the article appeared. Eventually I made things up with her: she started to like what I was turning into once I'd come to terms with who and what I was, and so we got back together on a more permanent footing. From a cynical point of view as well, if I had blown my career, either through physical damage or by alienating everyone, I couldn't have picked a more inopportune time: I was about to achieve a level of success I'd never dreamed would be available to me at this stage.

Before the end of 1986 I got involved in one of the unlikeliest recordings of my career: I appeared on a single with the all-girl heavy metal group Girlschool. It came about when their management asked if we'd mind them covering 'Leader of the Gang'. My immediate thought was that they were trying it on, because of all my songs that one is a bit sacred: there's only one Leader and there's only one Gang. I admired their pluck, though, so I told Jef I didn't mind. Later they rang to ask if I'd come to the session and help with the production, so I went simply because I thought it would be funny. When I met them I was stunned – they were absolutely brilliant musicians and keen Glitter fans, and I could see they'd take it seriously. But they squabbled like mad, so I ended up taking over the session, and through doing a guide vocal for their singer finished up in a duet. It turned out very well, but as it was on a tiny independent label I don't think anybody other than us ever got to hear it.

In 1987 we felt we'd consolidated all our hard work since 1983. Our live work now included far fewer colleges and about 80 per cent theatres and concert halls. That was a pity, because the universities had been so good to us, but their auditoriums simply couldn't accommodate the crowds the show was now drawing in. In many cases they couldn't afford us any more, either – the show had become more spectacular, so it was more expensive to produce, and because it sold out quickly we put our fees up. We were by then selling more tickets per tour than we had done in the seventies, so there was never a hint of putting the show on in small halls to make sure of a sell-out: at anything less than a three- or four-thousand seater we'd have to do two nights.

The advertising agencies were ringing up all the time that year, offering me massive fees to appear in commercials, but because the touring kept us financially secure we could turn them all down. Except, that is, the British Rail Young Person's Railcard campaign, which we did because, like the Heinz campaign, they gave us creative input. At the time Michael Jackson's plastic surgery had just been made public; it was well publicised, too, that Cher had had bits of her body chopped off, so I thought it would be funny to send the idea up – I also had Rod Stewart in mind, because he's very fond of Oil of Ulay and face packs! The cold cream one was actually very awkward to do: because make-up departments find it much easier to make up old skin if it's got a bit of a tan, I'd spent the day before under Jef's ancient sunlamp and come out looking like a boiled lobster! The cream was very soothing but on close inspection it's obvious that behind it I'm bright pink.

The campaign's tag line – 'Some people will do anything to keep hold of their Young Person's Railcard. Better luck next time, Gary!' – was an excellent angle for me, because the biggest problem for forty-year-old rock stars is how to grow old gracefully. I didn't want to be labelled the 'Peter Pan of Pop', because I knew I was old and didn't want to appear to be denying it. This series of adverts gave me the chance to send my age up, which I think helped a lot of people come to terms with how I saw myself in 1987. It was easy for me to do, too, because I've never been a great-looking guy, so I haven't got a pin-up profile or precious sense of vanity to protect. With these posters I felt as if I was saying, 'So what if you're old? You can still have fun' – which was very much in the original spirit of Glitter.

My fortunes continued on an upward curve through 1988, which was a spectacular year even by the standards I'd been setting. By the time it was over I'd had my own television chat show, I'd been on the cover of the *NME* and had taken up acting again. I'm sure a lot of this was because the people who were now becoming TV producers and senior journalists – people in their thirties – would have been in the original Gang. Those were the sort of people who would have been the first to notice my newly growing popularity, too, and must have figured it was safe to come out of the closet as Glitterfans. So just as the kids who had seen me in the universities had introduced me to the world of advertising, so these people were keen to put me in magazines and on television. The amount of media coverage I'd been getting went up drastically in 1988, and all of it was positive.

My chat show, on LWT's Night Network, was called *The Leader Talks* and was great fun to do. I had a big throne and would dress in Leaderish gear – very regal-looking with a bit of glitter thrown on. I had a hand in selecting the collection of very unusual guests, and we gave Julian Clary his first-ever TV appearance. I also got Noddy Holder from Slade to talk about the good old days; as well as Richard O'Brien, who wrote *Rocky Horror*. I thought the show worked very well, but the whole Night Network operation didn't go nationwide as quickly as it was hoped, so it was very underfunded and eventually had to shut down.

I'd like to do that again, because being an interviewer instead of an interviewee was so new to me that I don't think I gave it my best. I actually had some training for the job, because about four years previously a BBC radio producer with a sense of humour had asked me to present Radio 4's *Start the Week* while Richard Baker was on holiday. I turned up to go on air at eight o'clock in the morning, with half a dozen Special Brews and some speed inside me, and found that my guests included Salman Rushdie, Lady Antonia Fraser and Hayley Mills! I felt pretty intimidated even before the show began, and when I asked my first question to the author William Donaldson he fell asleep before I'd finished and didn't wake up for the rest of the show! I was thrown completely, but fortunately Mavis Nicholson, my co-presenter, was able to jump in and keep the conversation going. I recovered sufficiently to offer a contribution of my own later on and, surprisingly, the show's office got a few letters saying how much my approach had been appreciated.

That year, too, I took a dramatic role in the kids' TV series *How to Be Cool*. I was very nervous about it, but agreed because Roger Daltrey was in it and I thought he'd be able to look after me. Unfortunately, however, we weren't in any scenes together and nor were we ever at the studios at the same time, so I had to fend for myself. It wasn't a big part – I played an eccentric producer who ran a TV station – and because it had such a good cast and crew they got me through it. Jef's office got sent a lot of scripts for me to read after that; but the few films I fancied doing couldn't be financed, and all the others were either parts for ageing rock stars that were nothing more than a collection of clichés – the writers must forget that I know a lot more about rock stars than they do – or Glitter-in-space-fantasy ideas that weren't much better. The only project that interested us enough to go through with it was the play *A Slice of Saturday Night*. Although the six-month tour nearly killed me, and learning the lines was a bit of a problem, I really enjoyed the job and it formed a good acting apprenticeship. Also, other producers can't ignore the business it did – an average of 60 per cent in the theatres and 90 per cent in the rock venues. That has to be worth something with regard to future dramatic work.

I remain convinced that all these opportunities came about because the people who made the decisions were in the Gang – in each case they approached me to get involved. The 'Doctorin' the Tardis' single with KLF, who called themselves the Timelords for that particular record, is another example. They were both strong Glitterfans and really wanted to do something with me. They came to us and played us a rough mix which we liked; then I was so fascinated by their idea for using a police car in the video that I had to be in it too! It was entirely their personalities and the fact that they were doing something genuinely funny that persuaded me to appear in that clip. The guys behind Jive Bunny made us a good offer for performance footage of me to use in their Christmas video the next year – to go with their single that used large chunks of 'Rock 'n' Roll Christmas' – but Jef and I didn't like what they planned to do and so we turned it down. The Timelords was brilliant, though – Number One for six weeks. It not only put me back on *Top of the Pops*, but got me on the cover of the *NME* for the only time in my career! That was such a change from the seventies, when they only talked about me to run me down. I'll bet the editor there was one of the kids who had come to my show at his university five years earlier.

Our biggest triumph in that year was the live show; all the work that Jef and I had put into it since that summer at Ibrox Park was definitely coming together at this point. By then we'd completely outgrown the universities, and in order to make the show a bit more special we decided to go out only at Christmas – I've never understood why, but I've always been associated with Christmas, which is why 'Rock 'n' Roll Christmas' was so natural. We also devised a show that was more like a revue, with dancers, and me changing costumes several times. But the problem, which we'd had since 1972, was that the Glitterfans wouldn't tolerate any support act – if a group could just get them to stop shouting 'Leader! Leader!' for five minutes they were winning. So we hatched a plan in which Girlschool would actually come on and take over from my band during a song, then back me until the number finished, when I'd go off and leave them to do a short set. It worked, too. By the time the crowd had sussed out what had happened they'd got into what the group was doing and kept quiet. Their backing me for a couple of minutes also gave the impression that they were in the Gang, and so they must be OK.

That was the first tour to be called The Gang Show, a name which came about at a meeting Jef and I had over my kitchen table. It was so obvious that we didn't see it for a while, and we toyed with all sorts of clever-clever names for the tour before I suggested it. The timing was just right for that, too, because back then it wasn't old Glitter fans we were getting, but kids in their early twenties who were often coming to the shows for the first time, and they had to learn the responses. By 1988 they had done so – it actually takes a while, because it's really a process of mutual trust – and were ready to become the new Gang. I wanted to make them top of the bill, which is why I always ask my audience to applaud themselves and to bring people up to take photos looking from the stage, so they've got the Leader with his Gang solidly behind him.

The Gang Show was to be the Gang's show, and first time out it wasn't quite as slick as could be because we hadn't got the entrances and exits right or worked out how many dancers we should have. By 1989, though, it was firing on all cylinders, and that's when the old seventies' crowd started coming back to the shows in droves – even more so in 1990. By that time I had become hip again, and they realised nobody was going to laugh at them if they said they were going to see Gary Glitter. It was the old Gang joining up with the new Gang that gave us the numbers to move to the arenas – from the Hammersmith Odeon to Wembley or from the Manchester Apollo to the G-Mex.

Now all I've got to do is add a junior Gang to that lot and I'll be able to move into the stadiums. I believe it'll happen, too.

And There's More

I'm probably more relaxed at this time in my life than I've ever been before, which is only fitting after more than thirty years in rock 'n' roll. I live in a beautiful little village in Somerset, where – albeit seventeen years after it was offered – I've taken Rod Stewart's advice and live a life far removed from the pressures of celebrity. I'm just another member of the community, and so completely able to hang Gary Glitter up in the wardrobe when I get home that, maybe for the first time since I sold papers in Croydon market, I've got interests outside show business.

In 1989 I bought a boat and took up sailing, which I've found to be the perfect pastime: gently bobbing on the waves is the most brilliant way to unwind, and looking out to see absolutely nothing on the horizon is the ideal way to forget for a while any heavy workload looming up. Sailing appeals to my spirit of adventure, too. If I fancy a bit of danger I just take the boat out a bit further to where the waves are a lot taller – it can be risky, but nowhere near as heart-stoppingly scary as looking for women in the jungles of Bali! I keep myself fit and healthy, and since 1986 have stayed away from any stimulants other than life itself. I've even got my driving licence back – in spring 1991 I appealed against the ten-year ban and, as if I was getting time off for good behaviour, the court commuted it to five. Unfortunately Alison and I are no longer together, but at least we'll always remain the best of friends – and before we split up we had all but erased the memory of that awful Sunday in 1986.

Musically, I feel as confident now as I did all through the first half of the seventies. I'm working with a group of excellent young musicians led by the very capable Mark Pearson. My son Paul – who's becoming a first-class studio engineer and producer in his own right – is also getting involved in my work. Uncle John comes to see my shows whenever he gets the chance, which is a fantastic reward for me as I can show him that the music lessons he gave me nearly forty years ago haven't been wasted. Even my Mum sits through the occasional Gang Show and doesn't refer to my music as 'that racket' any more! I'm certain she doesn't understand it any more than she ever did, but I know she's incredibly proud of what I've achieved and vastly relieved that I've finally pulled myself together and settled down.

Apart from that, not much has changed. Gary Glitter is still larger than life, and everything he does has to be an event. My attitude to performance hasn't altered in spite of technological advances that allow artists to duplicate their studio work on stage. I'm still very much of the old school – James Brown, Otis Redding, Jerry Lee Lewis and so on – and believe that when fans buy a concert ticket they're paying for something very different from what they've already got at home. And I'll always remain aware that the primary function of my getting up on stage is to entertain them, not myself. I still can't get a record deal with a major company, either, even though I sell more tickets than almost any other British act – so nothing's changed there. In fact the only big difference between my approach to touring now and in the seventies – apart from the lack of truck drivers' specials – is that I know how to get what I want without ranting and raving like I had to on those early *Top of the Pops* programmes or on the MAM tour. I know how to make the deals, so I can put even more into the show with minimum fuss and expense behind the scenes.

And I'm still looking forward. *A Slice of Saturday Night* whetted my appetite for more acting work – I'd love a film part, but I know enough now to wait for exactly the right script. I'd like to be in there when the Eastern Bloc really opens up to western culture, for no other reason than that the tour title Glitter Over Moscow would have such a ring to it! I'd like to be able to sing some new songs once in a while, too, so Mark Pearson and I are concentrating on material that won't alienate any of the old Gang, but will be contemporary enough to bring in a new one. I'm sure my recording career will take off again, because I know that somewhere deep down I've got a couple of very good albums inside me. However, something else I've learnt is that this will only come about if I make it happen – waiting around for the music industry to wise up will take forever. I'd love to have another hit in America. And I'm determined to sail round the world – single-handed. Furthermore, I honestly believe that all these things are possible – especially with my Gang to back me up as they have done in the past.

Index

Index

Index